What We Could
Have Done with
the Money

What We Could Have Done with the Money

**50 WAYS TO SPEND
THE TRILLION DOLLARS
WE'VE SPENT ON IRAQ**

Rob Simpson

HYPERION

New York

Copyright © 2008 Robert N. Simpson

Library of Congress Cataloging-in-Publication Data

Simpson, Rob
    What we could have done with the money : 50 ways to spend the trillion dollars we've spent on Iraq / by Rob Simpson.
        p.   cm.
    ISBN 978-1-4013-2308-0
    1. Government spending policy—United States.   2. Waste in government spending—United States.   3. United States—Appropriations and expenditures.   I. Title.
    HJ7537.S47   2008
    336.3'90973—dc22   2008004439

Design by Meryl Sussman Levavi

FIRST EDITION

10 9 8 7 6 5 4 3 2 1

This book is dedicated to love of my life, my wife, Donna. Also to my friends and my family, especially my grandfather "Doc" Dougherty, a tough little Irishman who believed that having a drink and debating politics was about as fine a way to pass an evening as there could be.

CONTENTS

INTRODUCTION

In the time it takes you read this sentence, the war in Iraq has cost America another $50,000.[1]

When the total cost estimate first hit a trillion dollars, I happened to be watching one of the political talk shows. The question of "Why aren't people outraged?" was raised, and the answer was simply that most of us can't imagine how much a trillion dollars is. And so this book was born. It is, at its root, an effort to help us all appreciate just how much money that is. The hope is that by illustrating some alternatives, we can put the number in some sort of meaningful context.

But the book, frankly, seeks to do more than help you understand how much money we're spending. It was also created to provoke action.

This is our money. We could be doing great things with it—for ourselves and our families, for America and for the world. This is the sort of money that launches New Deals, that builds interstate highway systems, that pays for Marshall Plans.

My hope is that as you read this book, you will feel informed, enlightened, entertained, and amused. By the time you've finished it, you will almost certainly be appalled and angry. If that motivates you to ask candidates for office tough questions, to vote for change, to demand accountability from those we elect—not just during this election, but from this point forward—then it will have spurred you to become a better citizen, and one hopes that you will be rewarded with better government.

Now, hurry up and get reading. You've just blown another $800,000.

AUTHOR'S NOTE

A portion of the royalties from this book are being donated to Homes for Our Troops, a nonprofit, nonpartisan organization that assists severely injured servicemen and -women and their families by building homes or adapting existing homes for handicapped accessibility. For more information, visit www .homesforourtroops.org.

What We Could Have Done with the Money

- 1 -
HOMELESS FAMILIES
Solving the Problem
You Don't Even See

For most of us, the word "homeless" conjures up images of men begging for money on downtown street corners. Not families. But 600,000 families will experience homelessness this year, including more than a million children.[2]

That's a tragedy for them, but it's also a problem for the rest of us. Homeless children are more likely to be in poor health, to experience developmental delays, to develop mental health problems, and to exhibit behavioral problems. In short, they're much less likely to become law-abiding, productive citizens as adults.

Getting these families into stable housing is not just the compassionate thing to do, it's an investment in our collective future.

The reason we have so many homeless families is, quite simply, the lack of affordable housing. There is no place in America where a minimum wage job provides enough income for a household to afford the rent for a modest apartment. Even earning double the minimum wage won't do it.[3]

Five million American households spend more than 50 percent of their income on housing,[4] meaning they're one car breakdown or layoff or doctor's bill away from the streets.

The good news is, the solution here is simple and, in most cases, permanent.

When homeless families get housing subsidies, they very rarely find themselves facing homelessness again. (They are twenty-one times more likely to remain stably housed than comparable families exiting a shelter without a subsidy.)[5]

There are an estimated 15 million families in America who need assistance to pay for housing. Currently, about a third of them actually get the help they need. Section 8 vouchers provide

Invest $1 trillion in the stock market	$1,000,000,000,000
	X
Growth per year (Ibbotson forecast)	9%
	=
Total to be dispersed each year	$90,000,000,000
	—
Cost of housing vouchers for 10 million families	$68,050,000,000
	=
	$21,950,000,000

Maybe we could use some of the leftover money to help those men on the street corners (who include about 200,000 veterans).[6] Something to think about the next time you're downtown.

an average of $6,805 per year per family.[7] So to provide another 10 million vouchers would cost $68,050,000,000.

That's substantially less than we could earn on our trillion dollars, using Roger Ibbotson's market forecast. Ibbotson (Yale University, also Ibbotson Associates) is arguably America's leading market forecaster.[8] He calls for long-term market growth of 9 percent.

So we can get all those families into decent, stable housing. But the story is even more positive than that because the children of homeless families often end up in foster care. Nationally, the average cost of placing the children of a homeless family in foster care is $47,608, almost seven times the cost of a housing subsidy.

Of course, with the subsidy, the family actually stays together.

So a program to reduce family homelessness would be easily affordable, would keep families together, and save 1 million children a year from the litany of problems outlined above.

- 2 -

HABITAT FOR HUMANITY

A Place to Call Home

Say what you will about Jimmy Carter as a president, he's almost certainly the best ex-president we've ever had. As if global diplomacy, the Nobel Peace Prize, a Grammy Award, writing twenty-three books, and fund-raising for great causes weren't enough, he has made Habitat for Humanity one of the most well-known and successful assistance programs in history.

What makes Habitat so popular, I suspect, is that it's not about charity. It is the definitive "hand up, not handout" program. While disadvantaged people across America and around the world now live in homes built by Habitat, nobody gets a free ride. No one gets a Habitat home without contributing both their own money and sweat equity.

There's no denying the need. Around the world, about 1.6 billion people live in substandard housing, most of them in urban slums.[9] In America, the wealthiest nation in history, roughly one-third of us have housing problems, ranging from overcrowding to poor-quality housing to homelessness.

Most of them are working people who simply can't afford decent housing. (Our unemployment rate is usually around 5 percent, yet 33 percent of families have housing problems.) How about we use that trillion dollars to put a proper roof over their heads?

The average cost of a Habitat house in the USA is just under $60,000.[10] Which means that with a trillion dollars (and a lot of work from prospective home owners and Habitat volunteers), we could build housing for 16,666,667 families.

That won't completely solve the problem, because some 65 million people in this country have serious housing problems.[11]

Money spent on Iraq War	$1,000,000,000,000
	÷
Cost of average Habitat home in America	$60,000
	=
Number of families whose lives we could change	16,666,667

The average American family these days is 2.58 people, meaning that we'd actually be helping 43 million Americans. Now imagine that one in ten of them decide to help with future Habitat projects. That's an army of more than 4 million people helping their neighbors. Think of it as the biggest barn-raising party in history.

But it's one heck of a good start that could make one heck of a difference to our country in the years to come.

That's because home ownership has been proven to encourage families to get more involved in their community; it helps the working poor build wealth; and children who grow up in decent housing are healthier, do better in school, and stay in school longer.

All of which would make this country a better place to call home for all of us.

- 3 -

REBUILDING
NEW ORLEANS

Like We Mean It

People have referred to New Orleans as "the city that care forgot" for decades. It used to mean that life was carefree in the Big Easy. In recent years, though, the term has taken on a new and much sadder meaning.

While thousands of Americans have traveled to the Crescent City to help it rebuild, most of us assumed that government would somehow take care of it. Well, government hasn't.

There is much to fault in the rebuilding efforts—the Army Corps of Engineers, for instance, says that the levees "may be" rebuilt by 2011—but let's take the positive approach and think about what we might achieve with, say, a trillion dollars to spend.

Let's start by protecting New Orleans against another Katrina. A total of $8.4 billion has been allocated for the levees. The actual cost to rebuild the levees to withstand a category 5 storm could run to as much as $40 billion.[12] Fine. Do it.

Experts point to disappearing wetlands around New Orleans as one of the reasons the damage from Katrina was so severe, since each mile of wetlands reduces storm surge by several inches. It could cost up to $14 billion to restore coastal wetlands.[13] Do it.

We can put some architectural excitement into the city with the proposed New Orleans National Jazz Center and park. The plan would cover a twenty-acre area and include a new hotel, city hall, concert halls, an open-air park, a jazz museum, and studio and classroom space. A bold vision, with a preliminary price tag of $715 million.[14] Round it up to a billion dollars, and do it.

A proposal has been put forward for a Gulf Coast Civic Works Program, modeled on the Works Progress Administration in the

1930s, which would create 100,000 public jobs paying $15 an hour, to help residents get back on their feet and rebuild their communities.[15] Get them working forty hours a week for a year, and the total would only be $3 billion. Pay them a little more, cover the Social Security and Medicare costs, you're still getting

Rebuild levees	$40,000,000,000
	+
Restore wetlands	$14,000,000,000
	+
National Jazz Center	$1,000,000,000
	+
Civic Works Program	$6,500,000,000
	+
Houses for displaced families	$20,000,000,000
	+
Rebuild rental units	$5,000,000,000
	+
Public housing	$765,000,000
	+
Business subsidies	$20,000,000,000
	+
B-to-B ad campaign	$100,000,000
	+
Tourism ad campaign	$100,000,000
	=
Total	$107,465,000,000

Approximately $35 billion has actually been earmarked for rebuilding the Gulf Coast. Sadly, two years after the storm, only 42 percent of that money had been spent.

away with less than $5 billion. Add in some skilled tradespeople, who will earn more—maybe kick the total up to $6 billion. Throw in half a billion for supplies and we've probably covered the costs of getting power lines, water, and sewers working again.

Some 81,000 families displaced by Katrina still live in FEMA (Federal Emergency Management Agency) trailers.[16] Build them each a $200,000 house. Total spent—$16.2 billion. Heck, upgrade the appliances and put in granite countertops, you're still below $20 billion.

Some 33,000 rental units have been identified as needing to be rebuilt.[17] Let's ballpark $150,000 apiece for them. Approximate total cost, $5 billion.

New Orleans had about 5,100 public housing units.[18] At $150,000 per, that's another $765 million to rebuild them.

Looking beyond buildings, the area's economy is going to need a leg up. Maybe subsidies for opening new businesses on the Gulf Coast. Let's pluck a number out of the sky and dedicate $10 billion to that. No, $20 billion. Then let's spend $100 million on a business-to-business ad campaign to let people know about it. Speaking of advertising, how about another $100 million to encourage the tourists to come back?

Okay, I'm getting down to some relatively small stuff here. And the city that care forgot is starting to feel like the land of opportunity.

Total spent—$107,465,000,000.

And just in case you're inclined to quibble with some of the numbers, let's double that. We're now at $214,930,000,000.

Leaving us almost $800 billion to spend on other things. And leaving at least some of us wondering why this hasn't happened.

- 4 -

MORE COPS, SAFER STREETS

Go Ahead, Be a Streetwalker

I mean that in the nicest way. As in, you should feel free to walk the streets of your neighborhood or even downtown and feel safe doing it.

Is that too much to ask?

Most of us don't feel that way right now. There are parts of every city in America where you wouldn't walk around if you could avoid it. Or even drive through. Bruce Springsteen once sang about the part of town where you don't stop if you hit a red light. Ignoring the fact that perhaps Mr. Springsteen should have his driver's license suspended, he makes a good point.

No doubt, there are deep systemic problems within American society that lead people to a life of crime. We should try to solve them. Maybe some of the suggestions in other chapters (free college education, housing for the working poor, health care for all) could help us solve some of those underlying issues. For the moment, though, let's just attack the crime problem head-on.

Let's make it harder for criminals to do criminal things and get away with it. Maybe I've watched a bit too much *Law & Order,* but I'm thinking that more cops would help us do that.

So here's where I've gone with this one:

The median salary for a patrol officer in the USA is $46,596.[19] According to the Bureau of Justice, there are 663,535 police officers nationwide.[20] With a trillion dollars, we could have thirty-two times that many. Nothing scientific here, but I'm guessing that if your town had thirty-two times as many cops, you might see a decrease in crime. And yes, there would almost certainly be more donut shops.

Looking at it from a slightly more sensible side, we could dou-

New police hires	663,535
	X
Average salary for a police officer	$46,596
	=
Annual cost	$30,918,076,860
	X
Years and years of feeling safe	32
	=
Total cost	$989,378,459,520

We could even afford to raise the average police salary by just over $250 a year. Or, as a thank-you to the cops who've been keeping us safe to this point, we could give each of them a $16,000 bonus.

ble the number of police officers in every city and town in America, and cover the cost for the next thirty-two years. Something to think about the next time you hear a sound just as you're dozing off and wonder if it's someone trying to break into your house.

- 5 -

ELECTION CAMPAIGN SPENDING

Let's Buy Back Our Government

We appear to be knee-deep in the first billion-dollar presidential campaign in U.S. history. Of course, if you own a TV, or a radio, or if you're connected to the Internet, or if you read the newspaper, you probably figured as much.

The ads are everywhere. And gosh, but aren't they intelligent and informative? Performing a great service for democracy, don't you think?

Or do they strike you as insulting to your intelligence and an assault on the better principles of democracy? Based on a survey commissioned by the National Voting Rights Institute, I'll guess that your thinking leans more to the latter.

Politics is such a big-money game now that American voters overwhelmingly support limits in spending. Democrats, Republicans, young, old, urban, rural—every demographic, in every region of the country, wants the madness to stop. And yet it doesn't.

Which may contribute to the fact that seven in ten voters think large corporations have too much influence in politics, while two-thirds think ordinary voters do not have enough influence.[21] Two-thirds of voters also believe that spending limits will improve the honesty and integrity of elections.

Here's where it gets really crazy: voters firmly believe that campaign spending limits would cause candidates to spend more time on their official duties and talking about the issues, and that spending limits would allow ordinary citizens to be able to run for office.

Why, it's democracy gone wild!

I know all that stuff about duties and issues and ordinary citizens is pretty radical, but what do you say we give it a shot? We could even give this bold new experiment in government a catchy name, like maybe the American Revolution.

Even with presidential campaigns rolling out at a billion dollars, and gubernatorial campaigns spending tens of millions, and even congressional campaigns getting into seven figures now, we could easily afford to cover the cost with our trillion dollars. The interest alone would finance more campaigning than most of us can endure. (If we're covering the cost, we can set the limits, right?) So let's cover the cost of all election campaigning. Forever.

Suddenly, the people who are elected aren't beholden to big corporations or to big unions or to lobbyists—they're beholden to us!

It's a wacky idea, but it just might work.

Invest $1 trillion in the stock market	$1,000,000,000,000
	X
Growth per year (Ibbotson forecast)	9%
	=
Total to be dispersed each year	$90,000,000,000
	—
Total federal campaign spending (2004 election)[22]	$3,900,000,000
	=
	$86,100,000,000

Even during years with presidential elections, we could fund more campaign ads than any of us would want to see and still have tens of billions of dollars for other things. In non-election years, we'd have the entire $90 billion to play with. Let's cover the cost of state elections, as well. Let's fund some voter registration drives, to get more of us voting. Let's fund school trips to Washington, to educate and inspire our children.

- 6 -

THE ENTREPRENEURIAL SPIRIT

If the Government Helps You Start a Business, Is That Capitalism or Socialism?

Maybe we shouldn't get hung up on the labels. Instead, let's focus on the facts:

- Small business (defined as businesses with fewer than five hundred employees) accounts for roughly half of our GDP (gross domestic product).[23]
- Small businesses have generated 60 to 80 percent of net new jobs annually over the last decade. In the most recent year with data—2004—small firms accounted for all of the net new jobs. Yes, all of them.[24] Some large businesses grew, of course, but that growth was offset by large businesses that laid off workers.
- Nearly half of all small businesses, 49 percent, as of August 2007 had experienced no employee turnover during the previous twelve months. None.[25]
- Thousands of new businesses are founded in the United States each year, and over the last decade the rate of new venture formation has increased.[26]
- Due in part to downsizing at large firms and the rapid advancements in information technology, the trend toward more new business start-ups is likely to continue.[27]

There's always a flip side, though:

- Between 20 and 30 percent of new start-ups close during their first year of existence.[28]

So what have we got? A sector of the economy that accounts for half of our wealth and most of job growth. Due to the challenges and opportunities in the modern world, our economy will need this sector to expand, despite the fact that it's subject to a high rate of failure.

With a trillion dollars, we could have the largest pool of venture capital in the world. Got an idea for a business? Come on down!

The average solo start-up in America these days needs only $6,000 to get off the ground. Even in businesses started by a team of people, the average required is just $20,000.[29]

So we could fund more than 50 million new businesses. Given that there were 649,700 start-ups in 2006,[30] it would appear that we could significantly increase that annual number. For decades.

Obviously, we'd have to put some restrictions in place. We don't want everybody walking off the job to follow some crackpot scheme. So, sure, you've got to put some of your money into it. You've got to have some sort of plan. But plainly there's more than enough money there to ensure that if you've got a decent idea and a head on your shoulders, we can help you start a business.

Money spent on Iraq War	$1,000,000,000,000
	÷
Cost to start a new business	$20,000
	=
Number of start-ups we could fund	50,000,000

The Horatio Alger rags-to-riches story is deeply imbedded in the American psyche, but I still don't think that 50 million of us are ready to start our own businesses. So let's use some of the money to help those who do by hiring them some top-flight advisors. Let's also endow programs at universities and colleges so students can learn more business principles, tactics, and skills.

If we want to stay on top of the global economy, let's give ambitious, entrepreneurial Americans the money and the tools they need. That'll show the Chinese that we mean business.

- 7 -

CARING FOR OUR ELDERS

What Are We Going to Do About Grandpa?

One of our great fears as Americans is ending up in some government nursing home. All our money's gone, the staff is earning minimum wage and doesn't give a rat's ass about us, the food sucks, and the guy you share a room with snores and farts all night.

You worked your whole life for this?

Fact is, about four in ten of us will end up in a nursing home.[31] Ironically, four in ten Americans think it would be "totally unacceptable" to move into a nursing home themselves.[32] Let's hope it's not the same four.

If you're one of those four, your home may not be as bad as the one described above. It's worth noting, though, that a congressional report cited nearly one in ten nursing homes across the country for instances of serious abuse.[33]

There are alternatives. I suspect that as the almighty, self-obsessed boomers (I can say that because I am one) move into their senior years, we'll see more attention paid to those alternatives. Assisted living centers are a growing business, of course. Beyond that, projects like Green Houses hold great promise. First established in Tupelo, Mississippi, Green Houses brings seven to ten seniors together in a home that combines privacy and independence with visiting medical and custodial care. Boston's Beacon Hill Village has created community concierge service that helps seniors stay in their homes longer, with contracted caterers, house cleaners, drivers, plumbers, and other services—plus benefits like weekly lectures by notable Bostonians and exercise classes. New Hampshire has a program that pays families to take seniors into their homes and care for them.

All good, but some of us are still going to end up in the home. (Technically, "some of you," 'cuz I ain't going.) Let's make that life a little better.

Start with sprucing the place up. There are 17,000 nursing homes in America.[34] We could give them each a million dollars for capital improvements. A fresh coat of paint, new furniture, high-def TVs in the common rooms (heck, in every room), and some landscaping would make life a little nicer. A one-time cost of $17 billion.

We'll hire a chef to oversee the meals. One chef per home— a really good one. We'll pay them $200,000 each. Total cost, $3.4 billion per year.

Now let's give the nurses a raise. This should help us attract better people to work with our seniors, and help those people feel better about their jobs. Nursing homes average about one nursing employee per resident,[35] meaning there are about 1.6 million registered nurses, licensed practical nurses, and certified nursing assistants at work in nursing homes. Each of them gets a $10,000 raise right now. Total cost, $16 billion per year.

One common complaint is that residents in nursing homes feel disconnected from the community. How about a car and driver to take them to visit friends and family, or to church, or bingo, or shopping, or a show? Chauffeurs average a little under $30,000 per year.[36] You can lease a Mercedes E350 sedan for $579 a month, or about $7,000 per year.[37] One car and driver for every five residents should cover it nicely. After all, not everyone in the home is able to get out and about. So we'll need 320,000 cars and drivers, for an annual cost of $11.84 billion.

A top chef for every nursing home	$3,400,000,000
	+
Raises for nursing staff	$16,000,000,000
	+
Cars and drivers	$11,840,000,000
	=
Total annual cost to upgrade life at the home	$31,240,000,000

The Ibbotson forecast suggests that we'll see $90 billion in growth each year if we invest our trillion dollars. So we still have almost $60 billion a year to spend. How about massages once a week? Lessons in painting or pottery? Free airline tickets to go see the grandkids? Ask your parents what they think.

Now Grandpa's being cared for by a motivated staff and he's hanging out in a newly decorated place, watching a big-screen TV, eating fine-restaurant-quality meals, with his driver and Mercedes standing by to take him out to visit an old friend. Life in the home doesn't seem so bad now, does it?

And we're only spending $31.24 billion a year to do all that.

If we've invested the trillion dollars intelligently, we should be earning three times that much on it every year,[38] leaving us plenty of money to make things better for all the other seniors and caregivers across the country. But that's another story for another day. Right now, it's time to take my pills and have my nap.

- 8 -

AIR SECURITY

The Exposed Underbelly
of Homeland Security

Can someone somewhere please explain to me why we're taking off our shoes, removing our laptops from cases, and walking through puffer machines, x-rays, and metal detectors . . . only to climb aboard a plane the underbelly of which is filled with uninspected cargo?

If one of our goals in twenty-first-century America is to protect ourselves from terrorists (after all, that is, according to the current rationalization, why we're in Iraq), then might I humbly suggest that we inspect air cargo?

The Transportation Security Administration, or TSA, spends about $5 billion a year screening passengers and their baggage. And a paltry $55 million screening the cargo that can fly on the same airplane.[39] We have three hundred people charged with inspecting the cargo at America's roughly four hundred airports.[40] Sense a problem here?

Anyone who doubts that terrorists would put a bomb in a cargo hold might cast their minds back to Pan Am flight 103, which blew up in the air over Lockerbie, Scotland, for just that reason.

It should be noted that the House passed a bill that would require that all cargo loaded onto U.S. airliners be screened for explosives and all containers on U.S.-bound vessels be screened in foreign ports for radiation. Congressional budget analysts have estimated the House bill's cost at $21 billion over the next five years. President Bush opposed it, because of the cost.[41] (That cost, for the record, equals just over 2 percent of the money being spent on the Iraq War. In fact, proposals for fiscal year 2007 called for a total of $58.3 billion in spending on homeland security overall,[42] less than half of the $10 billion we spend each *month* in Iraq.)[43]

Of course, it's not as though there's no security plan in place now. The TSA relies on air carriers and freight forwarders verifying shippers and conducting their own screening and physical inspection. True, serious verification, screening, and inspection may interfere with efficient, on-time delivery and profitability, but surely all those companies will put your security ahead of their competitiveness and profits, right? So we just need to trust the airlines to do the responsible thing instead of the profitable thing. And they'll trust the 3,800 freight forwarders (with 10,000 branches) to do the same. And they in turn will trust the 1.5 million companies who are shipping material. And they'll all trust all of their employees.[44] That's an awful lot of trust for a post-9/11 world.

That's just one of the issues we're stumbling on. Isn't it reassuring to know that if someone on the consolidated terrorist watch list boards a U.S.-bound plane, U.S. Customs and Border

Invest $1 trillion in the stock market	$1,000,000,000,000
	X
Growth per year (Ibbotson forecast)	9%
	=
Total to be dispersed each year	$90,000,000,000
	—
Cost of proposed air cargo screening	$4,200,000,000
	=
Left for other homeland security initiatives	$85,800,000,000

Let's use some of that leftover money to make our ports more secure (less than 1 percent of sea cargo is inspected). And chemical plants (there are 15,000 of them, 123 in areas close to more than a million people). Power plants, railways, subways, stadiums—I could go on.

Protection (CBP) will know about it fifteen minutes after departure?[45] Yes, *after* departure. And, truth be told, CBP will only receive the passenger manifest at that point. It's up to them to then check the manifest against the watch list. Australia checks the list before issuing a boarding pass. Seriously, who wants to attack Australia, yet they have better security procedures than we do.

And of course if you fly out of a small airport, you can avoid bothersome things like federal agents, metal detectors, and puffer machines altogether.

I enjoy the theater of "security" at our airports as much as anyone, but if we're serious about protecting ourselves from terrorists, then let's get serious. Now might be a good time to start.

- 9 -

GIVING VETERANS THEIR DUE

Take Care of Those Who Take Care of Us

As we spend a trillion dollars on the Iraq War, budgets are being cut in other areas. The most shameful of these are the cuts forced on the VA and other care systems for veterans.

There's a sort of Mad Hatter logic to the thought that we're spending so much on a war that we don't have enough money to care for our veterans. So let's apply the same mad logic in the opposite direction: if we weren't spending all this money on the war, we could afford to give our veterans the care they deserve.

First, a quick look at the disgraceful state of the VA and other veterans' programs:

- Hundreds of thousands of Priority 7 or Priority 8 veterans are being denied VA care. Those already enrolled in VA care will be required to pay fees from this point forward, due to budget cuts. (Priority 7 or Priority 8 veterans are those who have the temerity to earn over $24,644 per year in civilian life.)[46]

- The compensation and pension claims backlog as of March 2006 stood at 582,204.[47]
- The number of veterans collecting unemployment insurance since August 2002 has risen by 96 percent.[48]
- Approximately 500,000 veterans experience homelessness in any given year;[49] approximately 194,000 are homeless on any given night.[50]
- The Bush administration hired PricewaterhouseCoopers to study shutting down at least eighteen major VA medical facilities.[51]
- At the Portland, Oregon, VA hospital, a sign instructs families that no more meals will be served to patients, and visitors should bring them food from home.[52]
- We all saw the disgraceful state of Walter Reed Army Medical Center when that story briefly ruled the news cycle.
- Even the National Cemetery Administration, which is also under the purview of the Department of Veterans Affairs, is underfunded to the tune of $50.9 million.[53]

It's no great surprise that things are so messed up when you learn things like the fact that the VA developed its fiscal 2005 health care budget without factoring in the new vets coming home from Iraq and Afghanistan.[54] Apparently they were anticipating the first war in human history without casualties of any kind. Hell, you can't get through a Little League baseball season without somebody getting hurt.

The real tragedy here is that it would take only a sliver of the trillion dollars to do right by our veterans. For example, House Resolution 2642 calls for an additional $500 million to properly maintain VA health care infrastructure, an additional $500 million for medical and prosthetic research, an additional $140 million to support efforts to improve the claims process, an additional $16 million to ensure effective oversight of VA programs and operations, an additional $165 million for the

Money spent on Iraq War	$1,000,000,000,000
	−
Additional costs for veterans' care, as detailed in H.R. 2642	$1,321,000,000
	=
	$998,679,000,000
	÷
Number of veterans in the USA[55]	24,500,000
	=
Amount for each veteran	$40,762.41

That doesn't seem like too much to thank someone for risking life and limb on our behalf. Surely anyone with a "Support Our Troops" ribbon magnet on their car would agree.

construction of extended care facilities.[56] Crazy, wasteful stuff, huh?

What to do with all the money left over? The simplest thing would be just to give it to the veterans. Let them make their own decisions about whether they'd like a new car, or to go back to school, or to put a down payment on a new house, or whatever the heck they want.

Here. For you. With our eternal gratitude.

- 10 -

GET OUT THE VOTE

Let's All Participate in
This Participatory Democracy

This is supposed to be what they call a "participatory democracy." For the last few decades, though, we've been a bit light on the participatory side of things. Our voter turnout numbers are, well, kind of pathetic. In the 2004 presidential election, only 64 percent of Americans over eighteen actually voted.[57] And that's for the MacDaddy of all votes. You don't even want to know what the municipal voting stats are.

We could rhyme off all the countries with better turnout than the USA, but it would take a lot of space to list all 138 of them. Yes, we rank a sterling 139th in the world in voter participation (out of 172). Our collective butt gets kicked by, among others, Trinidad and Tobago (66.2 percent), Burundi (75.4 percent), and Iceland (89.5 percent).

We like it when the USA is number one, right? Shouldn't we be number one in democracy? I mean, this is our game! (Yeah, yeah, the Greeks did it first, then the Romans, and most of the ideas for our democracy came from France. Try not to get hung up on the details.)

As with so many of the challenges we face, a trillion dollars might just help us in this, a little extra motivation to get more of us out to the polls. I mean, having a role in choosing the most powerful government in the history of the world is nice and everything, but a little extra spiff couldn't hurt, right?

Here's a thought: back in the early days of the current presidential campaign, there was a bit of flap about Barack Obama not wearing an American flag pin in his lapel. His response was that patriotism is not defined by a pin. But maybe, in a way, it could be.

What if we used a pin to show that you had voted, kind of

Money spent on Iraq War	$1,000,000,000,000
	÷
Eligible voters	213,244,291
	=
Value of each American flag pin to reward you for voting	$4,689.46

The lapel pin is just one possible reward. Maybe we could draw up a list of things (all with a patriotic theme) worth $4,689.46, and let voters take their pick: collections of the greatest American movies, music, or literature ever created, trips to Washington, trips to national parks to appreciate our natural wonders, trips to the Olympics to cheer on American athletes, portraits of great moments in American history, or portraits of great presidents—perhaps printed on small sheets of green paper.

like those stickers you get when you've given blood? Only way, way better.

I'm talking about a lapel pin in the shape of the American flag, with stripes of diamonds and rubies. And a field of blue sapphires for the diamond stars in the corner. We're talking about some serious Proud to Be American bling.

We have about 218,544,291 adults in the USA. Approximately 5.3 million are currently or permanently ineligible to vote, due to felony convictions.[58] So if we want full turnout, we'll need to reward 213,244,291 voters.

Meaning we could spend $4,689.46 on each pin. If that was the reward for voting, I submit that voter turnout of almost 100 percent would be almost inevitable.

One last thing: before you go, take a minute to find out how the candidates plan to spend your money.

- 11 -

FIXING MEDICARE

We Can't Save Medicare,
but We Can Save Lives

The pending crisis in Medicare doesn't get quite the media attention that Social Security does, but it's no less frightening.

We can start with a couple of irrefutable facts that set the groundwork: the retiree population will balloon as baby boomers age, and life spans are growing longer with each passing year. Net result: more people on Medicare, for longer periods of time.

Add to that the fact that new medical treatments, while saving lives and improving the quality of life for those who are ill, are increasingly expensive, so the amount we spend on each enrollee will rise.

All of which makes the future of Medicare a financial disaster trifecta.

Currently, Medicare's running a surplus. But come 2011, the scales tip, and it will shift to a deficit. By 2019, we'll have used up all the reserves and we'll be staring a crisis in the eye.[59]

Sadly, a trillion dollars wouldn't cover our needs for more than a few years. (Medicare benefit payments totaled $374 billion in 2006.[60]) What to do?

Well, if we can't increase the supply of money fast enough, let's see what we can do about decreasing the demand. The U.S. Preventive Services Task Force (a division of Health and Human Services) has recommended a core set of clinical preventive services. Primarily, they deal with cancer screenings, vaccinations, and the like.

A recent study showed that increasing the use of just five of those preventive services would save more than 100,000 lives every year.[61] Let's go for the entire core set, which would cost an average of $84 per year for women and $52 for men.[62] It would only take $20.5 billion a year to cover every man, woman, and

Invest $1 trillion in the stock market	$1,000,000,000,000
	X
Growth per year (Ibbotson forecast)	9%
	=
Total to be dispersed each year	$90,000,000,000
	−
Cost of all preventive screenings for every person in America	$20,500,000,000
	=
Money left over (every year)	$69,500,000,000

We still have almost $70 billion a year to spend. It may seem like a lot, but it breaks down to $190,410,959 per day, or about 65¢ for each of us. Go ahead, have a Flintstones vitamin on Uncle Sam.

child in America. Less than that actually, since kids don't need regular screenings for breast cancer, colorectal cancer, or chlamydial infection.

While the point of the screenings is to save lives, there's a financial angle, too. Six percent of Medicare beneficiaries account for 55 percent of spending,[63] largely because it becomes incredibly expensive to treat a condition once it's become catastrophic or life-threatening. So if we catch their diseases earlier, it might cost significantly less to treat them.

The investment earnings on our trillion could cover the cost of the preventive screenings for all of us, forever. Plus, we'll still have a trillion dollars in the bank to deal with shortfalls when they arrive. And we're saving 100,000 lives a year.

We may not have saved Medicare in this chapter, but that's not a bad day's work.

- 12 -

PRESCRIPTION DRUG PLAN

And Your Co-Pay Is . . . Zero

If you can prove you're a senior citizen.

It would be nice if the trillion dollars could cover the cost of all prescriptions for all Americans. And it could, for a little less than four years.[64] For a more long-term solution, though, we'll have to limit eligibility.

There's been a great deal written about the Medicare Prescription Drug Plan. Seemingly a well-intentioned effort, it tried to straddle that line between public and private systems and ended up confusing just about everyone. Apparently someone somewhere thought the world of prescription drugs wasn't confusing enough already.

So here's a simpler approach. Every senior in America gets every prescription paid for. Period. For "the greatest generation," it means no more worries about which plan covers what and what's not covered by anything and how much is the co-pay and can I really afford my meds this month?

I suspect that the insurance companies wouldn't mind, since it would mean that they no longer had to bear the burden of paying for prescriptions for that part of the population who gobble up drugs like there's no tomorrow. Of course, they gobble up those drugs because without them there might not be a tomorrow, so it's kind of hard to criticize them for it.

The insurance companies, being as dedicated to helping people as they are, would no doubt use the savings to give the rest of us a break on our drug costs and co-pays. Don't you think? Or they could be legislated into doing so. I'm just saying, that's an option.

The government would be free from the cost and complexities of the Medicare Prescription Drug Plan, and they would no

Invest $1 trillion in the stock market $1,000,000,000,000

                                                          X

Growth per year (Ibbotson forecast)   9%

                                                          =

Total to be dispersed each year $90,000,000,000

                                                          —

Prescription drug spending for those
over sixty-five[65] $69,478,200,000

                                                          =

Surplus—to save for future years,
when we have more seniors
and drug prices rise $20,521,800,000

Now, if it were up to me, I might put the surplus into starting
a new pharma company to develop cheaper drugs and break
what seems to be an oligarchy, but I'm rebellious that way.

doubt pass the savings on to us in the form of lower taxes.
Wouldn't they?

Of course, we may not be able to carry this on forever, because prescription drug costs in recent years have been rising
three times as fast as the general cost of living. Well, in this
country, anyway. Not so much in the rest of the world, strangely
enough. Which is not to suggest that pharmaceutical companies
have an unreasonable amount of influence on our government.
Or to go a step further and suggest that the high cost of drugs in
this country and the large campaign contributions that come
from drug companies are related—well, that would clearly be ir-
responsible and unfair.

What is fair is making sure that our seniors can get the drugs
they need to extend, and improve the quality of, their lives.

- 13 -

HOSPITALS IN THE MIDDLE EAST

A Healthier Way to Fight Terrorism?

Watching a report on the war one night, I was struck by a scene from a refugee camp. The father of a sick child was pleading with the video crew to do something to help his son. The pain and fear in his eyes would tear at the heart of any parent. Any *person*. It struck me that if the Americans there could save his child's life, it would probably be impossible for anyone to convince that man that America was his enemy.

That man, his child, and probably a lot of the people around them, would almost certainly not ever become anti-American terrorists.

What if America became the caregivers and lifesavers of the world? If we spent a trillion dollars building and operating hospitals, could we win over the hearts and minds of those who might otherwise turn against us?

While we may debate the health care system in America and lament that we lag behind most industrialized nations in many ways, the fact remains that our health care system is light-years beyond what exists in many parts of the world.

An examination of hospital projects throughout some of the world's trouble spots reveals not only a desperate need for better medical care, but also the fact that it's much less expensive to provide care there than it is here. A CURE International report in 2003 showed that the average cost per bed to build an orthopedic hospital in the USA was $1 million. In Afghanistan, it was $25,000.[66]

A look at various hospital construction projects throughout the Middle East and Africa reveals an average cost of $41.3 million to construct and equip them.[67] And generally you could add about 10 percent per year to run the facilities and cover the costs of patients who cannot pay for their care.[68] So to build and equip a hospital, and cover operational costs for twenty years, a figure of $125 million would seem reasonable.

Meaning we could establish and operate 8,000 hospitals in the Middle East or third world countries we feel might be breeding grounds for anti-American sentiments.

The average size of the hospitals we studied was 250 beds. The average stay in a hospital is a little less than a week. So our new hospitals could each serve 13,000 inpatients a year, plus emergencies and outpatient treatment. Even taking just the inpatients as a base number, that gives us 13,000 families each year per hospital who could be persuaded in a visceral and powerful way that America is their friend.

Hospitals we could build	8,000
	X
Patients per year, per hospital	13,000
	=
	104,000,000
	X
Years of hospital operating costs covered	20
	=
Patients served	2,080,000,000
	X
Family members and friends of patients (lowball guess)	5
	=
People the terrorists will probably never recruit	10,400,000,000

Have you spotted the problem here? There aren't 10 billion people in the world, let alone 10 billion potential terrorists. Maybe we don't need to build so many hospitals over there, and we could save some of the money for our own health care issues.

TV FOR ALL

Can We Have the Revolution Later?
I'm Watching *CSI* Right Now

There has never been a country where people had 200 TV channels to choose from that had any sort of civil war or revolution.

Is there a lesson to be drawn here?

With a trillion dollars, we could buy a satellite dish for every household on the planet. And still have a few hundred billion dollars left to pay for their programming. Check around online. Satellite dishes generally run about $300 in most countries. (Since a lot of countries are still struggling to get phone service throughout their nation, I'm assuming that wiring them for cable would be cost-prohibitive.)

A little cultural sensitivity would be needed, of course. Start pumping *Desperate Housewives* into fundamentalist Muslim areas, and there's going to be trouble. But *Afghani Idol*? It's a natural. *Funniest Home Videos* is a franchise you can replicate anywhere.

One of the few encouraging things about Iraq these days is the TV scene. There was an explosion (sorry, poor choice of words) of satellite dishes sold after Saddam fell. Now they're broadcasting sitcoms where children take adults hostage (oh, the zany antics!) and lifestyle shows where they do makeovers on homes that have been bombed (and no, I'm not kidding about that).

Sure, there will be broadcasters with a political agenda, including some who will be vehemently anti-American. The bet here is that they can be overcome with good old-fashioned lowest-common-denominator capitalist fare: sitcoms, soaps, cop shows, game shows.

Truth is, most people are more interested in being entertained and distracted from their problems than they are in

World population (from CIA *World Factbook*)[69]	6,602,224,175
	÷
Average number of people per household (estimate)	3
	=
Number of satellite dishes required	2,200,741,392
	X
Cost per dish	$300
	=
Total cost	$660,222,417,600

So we're left with just over a third of a trillion dollars to pay for ongoing subscriptions. Or, in some cases, for a TV. Maybe a La-Z-Boy chair, some chips and dip, a few sodas.

sucking up extremist political/religious dogma night after night. That's why NBC has better audience numbers than Fox News.

I could go on, but my favorite show's about to start.

- 15 -

MAKE THE WWW WORLDWIDE

The World Wide Web Isn't, but It Could Be

If you're trying to do business, connect with friends, learn something, or speak out on an issue, you will almost certainly turn to the Internet. In fact, most of us would feel crippled without it.

But most people in the world cannot access the Internet. In fact, there are still thirty countries with Internet penetration of less than 1 percent.[70] And there are more than eight times as many Internet users in the USA than on the entire African continent.[71]

So the hypothesis here is that if we made the www a truly worldwide web it could help the world in a number of ways. It would help poorer nations build their economies. It would help people in those countries become more educated (hello, University of Phoenix). It would help people around the world find each other, share ideas, and become more conscious of life beyond their own neighborhood. And the free flow of information and ideas tends to make life difficult for totalitarian regimes, which might just lead to a little more democracy around the world.

But is it achievable?

The big hurdle is that many homes and businesses in developing countries don't have electricity or phone lines. The cities and towns, though, do. We couldn't afford to wire every house, but we could easily afford to build WiFi clouds over every major city in the world.

The estimated cost of Philadelphia's WiFi network is $10 million.[72] So we could conceivably cover 100,000 Philly-size cities. Only, there aren't that many cities that big on earth. Philadelphia, with a metro population of just over 5 million, is about the world's 40th largest city.[73] By the time you get down to the 3,000th largest city (Purwakarta, Indonesia), you're dealing with a population of about 120,000.[74] So we'd be building WiFi clouds for much smaller cities. True, there's less existing infrastructure to build on, but then again, labor costs in Purwakarta are probably a lot lower than in Philadelphia. So let's just work with the $10 million.

We could build WiFi clouds for the 5,000 largest cities in the world for about $50 billion. Leaving us $950 billion to buy laptops so people have something to access the Internet with. Which could translate into 1,359,084,406 Dell Inspiron notebooks. Roughly one for every family on earth.

Welcome to the worldwide web. Hey, Akbar, have you seen Babatunde's FaceBook page? It's awesome!

Cost for citywide WiFi cloud	$10,000,000
	X
Cities with population over 100,000	5,000
	=
Total for WiFi installation	$50,000,000,000

Cost of Dell notebook	$699
	X
Number of families on earth[75]	1,320,444,835
	=
Total for computers	$922,990,939,665

So we could build the WiFi clouds and buy every family on earth a laptop for a grand total of about $973 billion. Worldwide web, indeed.

- 16 -

INTRODUCE IRAQIS TO THE REAL AMERICA

Take Them Out to the Ball Game

We want the people of Iraq to embrace American values, right? So why not take them to a ball game?

We fly them over here. Some go to Boston, some to Cincinnati, some to L.A., some to Phoenix. Put them up in a hotel, pay for their meals, cabs, souvenirs, and tickets to a major-league baseball game.

They get an up close and personal look at America. Probably

Baseball ticket for every Iraqi (27,499,638 Iraqis x $22.21 per ticket)[76]	$610,766,960
	+
Cost of return flight from Tehran to a U.S. city with a big-league ball team	$85,706,825,600
	+
Three nights' hotel	$3,391,691,500
	+
Incidentals and meals for 4 days ($1,000 each Iraqi)	$27,499,638,000
	=
Total cost	$117,208,922,060

We'd still have $882,791,077,940 left over. So maybe every American should go to Iraq for a soccer game, too.

meet some Americans whose main concerns in life are looking after their families, working to keep food on the table and a roof over their heads, and trying to be decent human beings. Which might just remind them of themselves.

Maybe they even pick up a thought about tolerance when they see fans of opposing teams actually getting along with each other. To see a Cardinals fan passing a bag of peanuts to someone in a Reds cap, to watch as a Dodgers fan lets a Giants fan go ahead of him in line—inspirational stuff!

- 17 -

BUYING PEACE

Pay Iraqis to Be Nice to Each Other

S uppose I offered to double your annual salary, and the only condition was that you had to be nice to your neighbor. I'm not saying you have to cut his lawn or wash his car—just wave hello in the morning and don't put a bomb in his driveway. Would you go for that? Is it possible that the folks in Iraq would?

Admittedly, they have some issues that run pretty deep. So let's up the ante and give them triple their income. Every year.

According to the U.S. Agency for International Development, the average Iraqi's annual income is about $1,500.[77] The population of Iraq is 27,499,638.[78] Now, that figure comes from the CIA *World Factbook,* and their record on Iraq is a little dodgy, but let's give them the benefit of the doubt on this one.

Take a trillion dollars. Invest it in the stock market. The American stock market. Yes, Iraq has a stock market, but I'm not about to invest a trillion dollars in it.

Using the Ibbotson forecast, we can assume we'll have $90 billion a year to dole out.

Divide that by Iraq's population, and you get $3,272.77. More than double the current annual income of the average Iraqi. That's in addition to whatever they're earning now, so they'd actually be taking home triple what they do now.

The plan is simple enough. Be nice, you live on easy street. Do something nasty, we turn off the tap and you get nothing. Operate on a zero tolerance basis. You so much as reference the fact that someone's a Sunni when you criticize his soccer skills and no more money for you. Complain that Shia don't know how to make a decent baked kufta, welcome to the poorhouse. And the first time you tell a joke that starts, "A priest, a rabbi, and a Kurd go into a bar," the bucks stop there.

We may still have some Iraqis who want to do each other harm. But we could set up rewards for snitching on the bad

Invest $1 trillion in the stock market	$1,000,000,000,000
	X
Growth per year (Ibbotson forecast)	9%
	=
Total to be dispersed each year	$90,000,000,000
	÷
Population of Iraq	27,499,638
	=
Annual stipend for each Iraqi	$3,272.77

The market may not always do that well, so some years we may only double their income. One thing's for sure—with their incomes dependent on the performance of our stock market, Iraqis would become about the biggest supporters of American capitalism on earth.

guys. You tell us who set the bomb, and the good-behavior salary he used to receive now goes to you.

I'd like to believe that most human beings, in Iraq or anywhere else on earth, generally want to live in peace. I'm just saying that a little cash incentive couldn't hurt.

- 18 -

AN IPOD FOR
EVERY HUMAN

Instead of Blowing Up the Casbah,
Let's Rock It!

With a trillion dollars, we could buy a new iPod for every person on earth. Okay, not the big one, just a nano. But still . . .

There are, according to the CIA, 6,602,224,175 people on planet earth.[79] We could actually afford to buy more iPods than we need.

And whaddya say we get Product (RED) nanos? Not only does everyone get to carry around a thousand of their favorite songs, it would also mean $65 billion to fight HIV/AIDS in Africa, since Apple donates $10 to that cause for each Product (RED) nano sold.

Money spent on Iraq War	$1,000,000,000,000
	÷
Cost of iPod nano	$149
	=
Number of iPods we could buy	6,711,409,396

Hmm, more iPods than people. What to do? Do the next 109 million babies born get an iPod? Does each iPod come with an iTunes gift card? What if we pay a little extra and get an American flag printed on each iPod, so everyone can always be reminded of where this cool toy came from? What if we build recording studios in third world countries, so they can share their music with us?

If you want to spread American culture and values, may I suggest that popular music might do it better than guns? And maybe some people would be just a little bit less inclined to blow up America if their favorite band lives there.

- 19 -

TAKE OVER THE WORLD THE REAL AMERICAN WAY

Buy It

Some people look at the Iraq War as empire building. Others disagree. I'm not going to take a side in that debate, but I will say this: if you want to build an empire, war seems like an inefficient way to do it.

Especially if you've got a trillion dollars in your pocket.

It's kind of hard to get reliable numbers on real estate in Iraq (though I've got to believe it's a buyers' market these days), so I played out this idea with an example a little closer to home.

Canada.

I'm not saying we could buy the whole country. Toronto real estate has gone through the roof. And Vancouver's no bargain, either. But the prairies have got to go pretty cheap. And as for the Atlantic provinces—we could start buying them up and not even notice that we've dipped into our trillion-dollar kitty.

The province of Prince Edward Island, for example.

We could buy every house in the province, and every acre of farmland, for a measly $6,882,345,686.[80] True, they'd still technically be part of Canada, but there are advantages to that. As Canadian citizens, they wouldn't be able to vote in American elections, for example, so we'd never wake up one day to find

Number of households in Prince Edward Island	50,795
	X
Average cost of a house	$104,988
	=
Total cost to buy every house in the province	$5,332,865,460
Total acreage of farmland	646,137
	X
Average cost per acre	$2,398
	=
Total cost to buy all the farmland	$1,549,436,526
Total of all houses and farmland	$6,882,301,986
Money left over to buy other parts of the world	$993,117,698,014

For a relative pittance, we've just taken over an island of rich farmland, with great ocean views and people with almost no guns at all. Tell me that's not a better plan.

that they'd voted in socialized medicine for the USA when we weren't paying attention.

Let 'em keep their liberal ideas. And consider this: if they ever swing too far to the left, we'll evict them. All of them. After all, we're the landlord for every person in the province. We'll just post a notice on the bridge to the island that tells them they have to leave by the end of the month.

Now, since we've got $993,117,698,014 left to spend, there's a state in northern Mexico I've had my eye on, and a nice island in the Mediterranean—Malta, I think they call it. Let's go shopping.

INVESTMENT ACCOUNTS

Everybody Gets a Piece of the Dream

A lot of people in recent years have been bemoaning the great division in America between the haves and the have-nots. There are certainly plenty of statistics to support the notion. Here are a few:

American CEOs and CFOs now make 364 times what the average worker makes.[81] In 2006, private equity and hedge fund managers made more than 16,000 times what the average full-time worker makes.[82] The richest 1 percent of Americans enjoy net wealth 190 times that of the median household.[83]

Yes, the rich are indeed rich. And the disparity has grown over the past few decades and gives every indication that it will continue to grow.

A couple more stats:

The wealthiest 1 percent of Americans own 37 percent of all domestic stocks held by individuals.[84] The top 10 percent own 79 percent of all stock (both 2004 figures).[85] That leaves 90 percent of the country owning not much of anything. But we can change that.

We can give every living American $3,293 to invest in the stock market. (Yes, even the way-too-rich-already 1 percent will get $3,293. Though they may or may not take the time to open the envelope or cash the check.)

Those who already own stocks will certainly benefit, as an injection of a trillion dollars into the market can only help stock prices rise. And for the rest of us, it will mean we're finally in the game.

That could have a real effect on the inequity of American wealth. While the median household income in America has only grown 0.7 percent per year through the last twenty-five years, stocks have averaged almost 12 percent growth per year.

Money spent on Iraq War	$1,000,000,000,000
	÷
U.S. population[86]	303,681,455
	=
Amount we each get to invest	$3,292.92

Can't you see it now? Copies of *The Wall Street Journal* lying around the auto body shop, punks debating price/earnings ratios with their tattoo artists, your cabdriver on the phone with his broker? George W. Bush once said that he wanted to create an "ownership society." Well, here it is.

Which, gosh, may be a bit of an insight into why the gap between rich and poor keeps growing. It's not earning that makes you rich. It's owning. So let's all be owners. And while $3,293 may not seem like a lot (if you're a 1 percenter), consider that for a family of four, that's $13,172. And if you're among the 90 percent, I suspect that suddenly having more than $13,000 in the stock market would feel kind of significant.

It might even have an effect on our collective retirements. If a couple invested $6,600 in the stock market, and it grew at the 12 percent rate it's been averaging for the last quarter century, and they had thirty years to go until retirement, they would find themselves with an extra $197,735.49 for their retirement.

For those of us in the 90 percent, that's real money. That's something to dream about.

- 21 -

SOCIAL SECURITY

We Can Fix It, Just Not for You

Sorry. A trillion dollars is a lot of money (a *lot* of money), but it's not enough to dig us out of the Social Security hole we're digging for ourselves. Not even close.

The 2007 OASDI (Old Age, Survivors, and Disability Insurance) trustees report cites $4.7 trillion as the amount it will take to keep Social Security solvent for the next seventy-five years.[87] That may scare you, but not as much as it should. It means that you could fix Social Security if you threw $4.7 trillion at it right now. In 2005, a mere $3.7 trillion could have set things right.[88] Wait two more years and it wouldn't seem unreasonable to guess that it would take $5.7 trillion.

This may be the one instance where a trillion dollars feels like a token gesture.

Don't get me wrong. A trillion would be a great start, and it would certainly postpone the crisis. At least until after my retirement. But let's look to the longer term and the greater good.

Could a trillion dollars provide any sort of real and permanent solution? Yes, it could. Just not for you and me. Senator Jeff Sessions (R-Ala.) has proposed Portable Lifelong Universal Savings (PLUS) accounts that would start with a contribution from the federal government of $1,000 to each baby born in the USA. Interesting idea, Senator, but let's think bigger.

Take the trillion dollars and invest it. Use the earnings to fund accounts for each newborn. Let it grow. Problem solved.

The USA can expect about 4,242,000 births this year.[89] Next year, the number will rise slightly, but let's use that as a working number for now.

That paltry return that Social Security currently gets on its investments (4.823 percent) would generate only $48.23 billion to disperse in the first year. Only $48 billion. Don't federal government numbers boggle your mind?

Split $48.23 billion among 4,242,000 newborns, and each baby gets $11,369.64. If that earns 4.823 percent throughout the life of the person, by age sixty-five each of them would be sitting on $242,898.44. Not an insignificant sum, but as your financial advisor will tell you, that's not enough to retire on. So here's hoping that those kids still contribute to 401(k)s. And that there's still something left of Social Security by the time they get to their golden years.

However, if we could average the kind of return that the market has averaged for the past quarter century (12 percent), then each kid can start with $28,288.54 and celebrate their sixty-fifth birthday with $44,748,863.23. At which point, the whole idea of a monthly stipend from the government seems kind of quaint.

Let's take one more run at the numbers. This time, using the Ibbotson forecast of 9 percent long-term growth. Invest our $1

Invest $1 trillion in the stock market	$1,000,000,000,000
	X
Growth per year (Ibbotson forecast)	9%
	=
Total to be dispersed each year	$90,000,000,000
	÷
Babies born per year	4,242,000
	=
Each baby's account starts with	$21,216.41

That's nice, but it's the magic of compounding that makes it great. With compound growth of 9 percent per year for sixty-five years, we get to a retirement-day total of $5,746,378.99. And that's for every child born in America. Oh, baby.

trillion and give each of the 4,242,000 babies an account with $21,216.41 in it. By age sixty-five, it's worth $5,746,378.99.

Now, all of this does you and me no good at all. But maybe it convinces you to open an investment account for your children or grandchildren the moment they're born. As for yourself, start throwing money at your 401(k)s and IRAs, and start grilling candidates for any federal office about what they plan to do to solve this. Because when a trillion dollars won't solve the issue, you've got a big problem.

- 22 -

AMERICA'S BIGGEST LOTTERY

You May Already Be a Winner

M illions of us buy lottery tickets. Tens of millions of us when the jackpot gets big.

So what if we all won on the same day? That trillion dollars is certainly bigger than any lottery jackpot. Bigger than all lottery jackpots combined, I suspect.

Let's have a lottery with the Mother of all Grand Prizes—a billion dollars. That's enough to buy you some incredibly cool toys, like, say, a major-league sports franchise. And you'd probably still have a few hundred million dollars to play with.

And how about 1,000 second prizes of $1 million each? Sounds pretty exciting, doesn't it? And we've only used up $2 billion. That still leaves us $998 billion to be divided among the lesser prizes. We'll have 303,680,454 of those, just to make sure that everyone wins.

So the smallest amount you can win is $3,286.34. A family of four will walk away with at least $13,145.36.

Money spent on Iraq War	$1,000,000,000,000
	—
Grand prize	$1,000,000,000
	=
	$999,000,000,000
	—
1,000 second prizes	$1,000,000,000
	=
	$998,000,000,000
	÷
Number of people who win third prizes	303,680,454
	=
Amount that people not as lucky as you win	$3,286.34

Another way to go would be a lottery with a million prizes of a million dollars each. That would mean that 1 in 300 Americans would become an instant millionaire.

What are you going to do with yours? And what effect will all this winning have on America?

If we all went shopping, and spent all $998 billion that was earmarked for the small prizes, it would leave Thanksgiving weekend looking like a weak sales day at the mall. "Black Friday" is usually good for about $8 billion in retail sales. A pittance. We could shop like Black Friday every day for four months.

That would have to be good for America's retailers. And if we shop according to Thanksgiving weekend patterns, it would be especially good for the electronics, book, and clothing industries. And probably good for the employment picture, since all those industries would need extra help.

Not that it matters to you. You just won the billion-dollar grand prize, right?

- 23 -

CREDIT CARD DEBT

Pay Down the Plastic

The scary stories have been floating around for some years now. The average American household is carrying $9,300 in credit card debt.[90] That's a daunting stat, except that you probably know that you don't owe that much, so it leaves you feeling a little bit worried about the other guy and a little bit smug about your own financial good sense.

I'm guessing you feel that smugness because surveys show that 90 percent of Americans believe they have less credit card debt than that.[91] Which might suggest that we're collectively delusional, but the truth is, we're not. The $9,300 number is misleading. It is the average debt, but not the median. The number gets skewed by a relatively small group of households with staggering debt loads.

A number that gets us closer to the truth of the matter is the median credit card debt of $2,200.[92] Half of American households with credit card debt have less than that, and half of us have more than that. Still, $2,200 is nothing to sneeze at. And our debt is growing.

So let's stop it.

Total credit card debt in the United States has reached $665 billion on bank cards and about $105 billion on store or gas cards.[93] Grand total—$770 billion. We could use the trillion dollars like a great national home equity loan and pay off our credit card debt in a flash.

We'd even have $230 billion left over. If I might rant for a moment [Ed.—"for a moment"?], let's use some of that money establishing consumer economics courses in schools across the country. It's one of the great failings of our school system that we don't do more to teach our children about money—how the awesome power of compound interest can be your best

Money spent on Iraq War	$1,000,000,000,000
	−
Cost to pay off every bank credit card in America	$665,000,000,000
	=
	$335,000,000,000
	−
Cost to pay off every gas credit card in America	$105,000,000,000
	=
	$230,000,000,000

Nice to pay off everybody's plastic, but what about those without credit card debt? That's 55 percent of U.S. households.[95] We could split that last $230 billion between them, as a reward for being so responsible. So each household with no credit card debt gets a check for $2,046.94.

friend or your worst enemy, how home ownership is as much about tax deductions and equity growth as it is about a place to live, how one dollar invested when you're twenty could grow to $538.77 by the time you reach retirement (assuming stock market growth based on the past twenty-five years), etc. We could change the course of our children's lives with a little bit of basic money education. Okay, I'm done now. Let's get back on track.

Doing this would almost certainly reduce the number of personal bankruptcies in America. In 2005, 2.39 million U.S. households filed for bankruptcy, a 12.8 percent increase over 2004.[94] According to the American Bankruptcy Institute, filings dropped considerably through the first half of 2006 (most recent statistics available), but erasing all credit card debt would probably drop the rate to near zero.

So everybody's nagging debt gets paid. We virtually eliminate consumer bankruptcies. And, in all likelihood, the next day every restaurant in the country is full because now we all have no balance on our cards. Let's go out to dinner! Let's go shopping!

Ah, well. Being debt-free was nice for a minute there, wasn't it?

- 24 -

PAY FOR THE BUSH TAX CUTS

Even the Worst Cuts Can Be Healed, Can't They?

You may not have felt it at the time, but when the Bush tax cuts took effect, your life changed in a significant way.

You used to live in a country whose federal government was running a surplus. It was actually paying down the debt that was created through the years of voodoo economics. Then along came those tax cuts. Suddenly, you were living in a country that was getting deeper in the hole with each passing day.

I'm sorry to say that even a trillion dollars isn't going to set things right. The Center on Budget and Policy Priorities has calculated that over the ten-year period from 2005 through 2014, the direct costs of the enacted and proposed tax cuts would total $2.8 trillion.[96] Losing that kind of revenue can take a government from surplus to deficit in a big way.

So now the deficit grows bigger with each passing year. Which of course means bigger interest payments. Between 2005 and 2014, we'll pay an additional $1.1 trillion dollars in interest thanks to those tax cuts.[97] And by 2014, the interest payments alone will have grown so much that they'll equal what the government now spends on the Departments of Education, Homeland Security, the Interior, Justice, and State combined.[98]

Money spent on Iraq War	$1,000,000,000,000
	−
Interest we'll have to pay on the $2.8 trillion in debt created by the Bush tax cuts	$1,100,000,000,000
	=
Shortfall	($100,000,000,000)

So we can't even pay the interest, let alone pay for the tax cuts themselves. Here's another interesting, albeit depressing tax cut/deficit note: from 2001 to 2006, the typical middle-income American received a tax cut totaling $1,855 per family member (over the six years). But that family's share of the national debt burden grew by $8,936 per person.[99]

There's a natural temptation to blame deficits on that old bugaboo "big government." But that's not actually the problem here. Spending by the federal government, measured as a share of the economy, is actually below the average of recent decades.[100] But while spending may be down a little, revenue is down a lot. To its lowest level in forty-five years, in fact (measured as a share of the economy).[101] Though it may not seem like it when you look at your paycheck, we pay less in taxes than almost any other developed nation (as a percentage of GDP).[102]

The time will come when we actually have to pay for those things like education and homeland security. For now, even with a trillion dollars, the best we can do is pay the interest for a decade or so. It's a bit like an interest-only mortgage on the country. It'll buy us some time, but it won't buy our way out of debt.

- 25 -

ANOTHER LOOK AT
THE TAX CUTS

How About a Tax Cut for the Rest of Us?

Ah, the Bush tax cuts. What fun with math! There's a way to spin them for every political persuasion. One thing is certain: the tax cuts will cost the federal government more than the war in Iraq will. About $2.8 trillion, plus interest.

And yet somehow you probably don't feel $2 trillion richer.

The reason the tax cuts didn't make you feel rich is, quite simply, because you're not rich. Households with incomes in the top 20 percent received 70 percent of the tax cuts.[103] For example, if your income was over $1 million, you'd have received a tax cut of over $100,000.[104] So if you were rich before the cuts, you'll feel richer now. If you weren't rich to begin with, well, not so much.

Let's, for the moment, ignore the macro issues like what this does to the federal budget. Don't concern yourself that the Economic Policy Institute declares that the cuts "will make balancing the budget impossible" and that extending them "would make matters worse, indefinitely delaying any hope of balanced budgets" or even that "under reasonable assumptions, the tax cuts push the deficit to unsustainable levels."[105]

Sure, it's true that the trillion dollars being spent on Iraq could go a long way toward minimizing the scary deficit numbers. But forget all that.

This is all about you.

And if you're in a household that ranks in that lower 80 percent (you know, the ones who got less than a third of the tax cuts), here's a plan you might like. Let's take that trillion from the war and turn it into a tax cut for you.

I'm not going to get into complicated progressive tax scenarios here. This is like those flat-tax schemes you hear about every now and then (usually about once every four years, from

Invest $1 trillion in the stock market	$1,000,000,000,000
	X
Growth per year (Ibbotson forecast)	9%
	=
Total to be dispersed each year	$90,000,000,000
	÷
Number of households in the lower 80 percent[106]	92,808,800
	=
Each household's tax cut	$969.74

Not bad, huh? And I'm not even running for office. Actually, if I was, I'd probably suggest that we pay down some debt and start working toward balancing the budget. Which, in short, is why I would never get elected.

a third party candidate who doesn't stand a chance of getting elected, so he's free to propose just about anything). It's like that, only in reverse. Every household in the lower 80 percent gets a check for $969.74. This year. Next year. Every year.

You're welcome.

- 26 -

SOLAR POWER

Is It Wrong to Call It a Bright Idea?

In spite of its history as a lib-left-green-granola issue, this should be something we can now all agree on. Less dependence on foreign oil would be good for America, right? Exporting energy instead of importing it would be good, right? Fewer coal mines and less pollution would be good, right? High-tech, high-pay jobs—also good?

Okay, then. A few core stats: The sun pumps out more energy in one hour ($4.3 \times 1,020$ joules) than all of the energy consumed by all of human endeavor in one year.[107] The World Bank estimates that the global market for solar electricity will reach \$4 trillion in about thirty years.[108]

And a few other interesting facts: If you were searching for a perfect place to build large solar installations, it would be hard to do better than the American Southwest (where, incidentally, we're seeing massive population growth). New developments are making solar more efficient than ever—silicon nanoparticles applied on top of solar cells can increase power, transparent glass windows can now be used to generate electricity, and parabolic troughs make large-scale solar more productive than traditional flat panels.

Money spent on Iraq War	\$1,000,000,000,000
	÷
Cost to build a 10-megawatt solar plant	\$80,000,000[109]
	=
Number of plants we could build	12,500
	X
Homes a 10-megawatt plant can power	6,000[110]
	=
Total number of homes running on solar power	75,000,000

That would leave about 39 million homes (one-third of us) relying on more traditional methods of power generation.[111] Coal, our leading source of power, currently supplies 51 percent of our electricity.[112] It's also the dirtiest way to generate power. And with this much solar power, we can say goodbye to coal forever.

How much impact could we really have on America's energy picture with a trillion dollars dedicated to solar power?

The short answer is, we could supply all of the electricity needs for about two-thirds of American homes.

You'd want very much to be living in one of those homes, since once the plant is built, solar power is about as close to free as you can get. And, oh, how green you'd feel! Currently, your home is responsible for about 22,000 pounds of carbon emissions—two-thirds of that is from the electricity you use.[113]

There really is a light at the end of the energy crisis tunnel. It's the sun.

- 27 -

ETHANOL

There's Gold in Them Thar Prairies

Some people will tell you that ethanol is the answer to our oil needs and our environmental problems. Others say it's at best a partial solution, and one that brings problems of its own.

Ethanol is a high-octane fuel (the 2007 Indianapolis 500 winner ran on pure ethanol)[114] that burns cleaner than gasoline and reduces greenhouse gases. It's made from renewable resources (usually corn) and we already use enough ethanol to reduce our oil imports by 3 percent per year.[115] Currently, we just don't produce enough ethanol to make a more significant difference. So let's build more plants and produce more ethanol.

Aside from reducing our dependence on foreign oil and improving the environment, a massive program to build ethanol plants would be a boon for rural economies. Because transporting massive quantities of corn is expensive (and has some environmental issues of its own), it makes sense to build plants close to where the corn is.

A new 40-million-gallon-per-year plant would cost about $60 million to build, and is estimated to expand the local economic base by $110 million each year. Tax revenue for local and state governments will increase by at least $1.2 million a year. And nearly 700 permanent jobs will be created in the area near an ethanol plant.[116]

Let's build a thousand of them. That could reduce our oil imports by 30 percent.[117] And do great things for the air, for rural communities, and for the collective tax base. And if we build them like the Brazilians do—using waste from the process to power the plant itself—they'll actually generate a surplus of electric power as they produce the ethanol. Which could reduce the amount of coal we burn, which would also help our air quality. Those crazy Brazilians even turn the plant's wastewater into fertilizer.

Now, having $940 billion left to spend, let's go a step beyond. While corn ethanol reduces greenhouse gas emissions by 20 to 30 percent, cellulosic ethanol can reduce them by up to 80 percent because less fossil fuel is used to create it.[118]

Because cellulosic ethanol is created from fast-growing plants like switchgrass, as well as crop residues, industrial wastes, and municipal solid waste, it has the added benefit of not diverting land use from growing food. (Two-thirds of what goes into our landfills now contains cellulose.[119]) A commercial-size biorefinery would cost "between $200 and $250 million to build," says Brent Erikson, vice president of the Biotechnology Industry Organization (BIO).[120]

Let's get that party started with a thousand of those plants, too.

Of course, we'll have to convert our cars to run on E85 (fuel that's 85 percent ethanol/15 percent gasoline). There are about 140 million cars in America,[121] and the conversion cost is about $150 each.

In all, we've spent about $330 billion here. And potentially cut our oil imports by 60 percent.[122] At which point, as long as we keep producing some oil domestically and we stay friends with Canada (which is actually our largest foreign supplier), we should be covered. Hey, OPEC, I got yer oil embargo right here.

1,000 conventional ethanol plants	$60,000,000,000
	+
1,000 cellulose ethanol plants	$250,000,000,000
	+
140,000,000 E85 conversion kits	$21,000,000,000
	=
	$331,000,000,000

This would give us cleaner air, less dependence on foreign oil, productive use of industrial and municipal waste, and boom times for rural America. And we only spent a third of the money.

- 28 -

LET'S GET AMERICA DRIVING HYBRIDS

or, The Sound You Don't Hear Is Your New Car

Oh yeah, that'll happen. 'Cuz deep down, we're a nation full of Ed Begley, Jrs., right?

True, hybrid vehicles can reduce air emissions of pollutants like nitrogen oxide, hydrocarbons, and lead by up to 90 percent, and cut carbon dioxide emissions in half.[123] All of which has helped to convince over half a million Americans to buy hybrids.[124] It's also true that when the battery is running the vehicle, it's silent. Which is not all that important, but it is kind of cool.

To persuade everyone to get a hybrid, maybe we should look at a big, obvious, simple way to put money in your pocket. Let's face it, when you're dealing with human beings, recognizing the power of self-interest goes a long way.

So consider the Toyota Camry—the most popular sedan in America. The hybrid model costs about $5,000 more than a standard gas-engine model. Let's flip that. Make the hybrid $5,000 less expensive.

To do that, we'd have to subsidize the cost of the Camry hybrid to the tune of $10,000. So let's do it. In fact, let's offer a $10,000 subsidy on every hybrid vehicle sold in America. There are now hybrid models ranging from subcompacts to SUVs. There's even a hybrid Porsche in development.

And while the subsidy will save us all money on the purchase price, we'll also save money every time we drive. Back to the Camry as an example—the gas engine gets twenty-one city mpg; the hybrid gets thirty-three.[125]

Overall, hybrids will use about 10 percent less gas than a stan-

Money spent on Iraq war	$1,000,000,000,000
	÷
Subsidy on each hybrid vehicle	$10,000
	=
Total number of hybrids	100,000,000
	÷
Number of new vehicles sold in America annually	17,000,000[126]
	=
Years the program could run	5.88

Little known fact that might make hybrids even more appealing, at least to those with a need for speed: with many hybrids, when you want to accelerate really quickly, both the gas and electric motors kick in. Thus, even though the Highlander Hybrid is a big, comfy SUV, it's the fastest vehicle Toyota makes.

dard vehicle. The USA uses about 56 billion gallons of gas per year to power our cars and other light transportation. With the number of vehicles we can afford to subsidize, about 40 percent of the passenger vehicles in America could be hybrids within a few years.[127]

So we'd save more than 22 billion gallons of gas per year. And be putting fewer pollutants in the air. In short, we'd have a quieter, cleaner nation that has more money in its pockets, and is less beholden to the world's oil producers. A good thing? Ya think?

- 29 -

REDISCOVERING TRADITIONAL AMERICA

Take Me Out to the Ball Game

What better way to affirm traditional American values than to take everybody out to a ball game?

We could do it for less than $7 billion, based on the average ticket price at a major-league ballpark ($22.21, if you're curious). But nobody just buys a ticket and watches the game, right? You need snacks and drinks and souvenirs. You've got to pay for parking. And, as any good barker will remind you, you can't tell the players without a program.

So let's pile on the nachos and peanuts and Cracker Jack. Let's buy ball caps and programs. Let's pay for everybody's parking. And with all that in mind, let's call it $100 per person to really do it right at the old ball game.

There are about 303 million of us these days, which means we'd spend about $30,300,000,000. Mere pocket change when you've got a trillion dollars.

To spend the entire trillion dollars, we'd have to take every American out to thirty-three games. That's an awful lot of baseball, so maybe we should look at some other sports, as well.

Average price of a major-league baseball ticket	$22.21
	X
Population of USA	303,681,455
	=
Total cost	$6,744,765,115.55

Let's look beyond the majors and support minor-league ball, too. (Go, Dayton Dragons!) And let's build more diamonds for kids to play on. Heck, let's have JumboTrons at Little League diamonds. And while we're at it, let's build baseball diamonds in Iraq.

We could buy every American a ticket to an NFL game, an NBA game, and an NHL game for a mere $40,974,690,000. Let's round up that number to a hundred billion, to cover some of the incidentals.

We've still got almost $870 billion left to spend. So . . . who likes college sports? Soccer? Beach volleyball? Pro bowling?

- 30 -

MAKEOVERS FOR ALL AMERICANS

You Look Great! Have You Lost Weight?

We're an ugly bunch. Really. Walk down any street, walk through the mall, walk up to a mirror if you don't believe me.

But cut yourself a little slack. It's not all your fault. Well, okay, the supersize McFatty meal you had for lunch—that's on you. Literally. But as a people, we're suffering from too much food, too much stress, not enough exercise, and not enough sleep—it all takes its toll.

Sometimes, you don't know whether to envy movie stars and their endless good looks or just resent the hell out of them. I mean, George Clooney is forty-seven years old. Annette Bening is fifty. Richard Gere is almost sixty. Goldie Hawn is sixty-two. It's just not fair.

So in the interest of fairness, and in helping us all to feel better about ourselves, let's consider using the trillion dollars to give the whole country a makeover. One like the stars get. Skin toning, waxing, plucking, seaweed body wrap, massage—the works. We can even get it where they do, at Thibiant Spa in Beverly Hills. Aida Thibiant is known as the "Face Saver to the Stars." (*In Style* magazine reported that Ms. Bening indulges herself at Thibiant Spa, so you know it must be true.)

Let's give every American the full treatment. Thibiant's Ultimate Spa Sanctuary includes collagen facial, hand spa, décolleté

Money spent on Iraq War	$1,000,000,000,000
	÷
Cost of Thibiant's Ultimate Spa Sanctuary	$500
	=
Number of total spa treatments we could afford	2,000,000,000
	÷
80 percent of Americans who could probably benefit from a spa visit	240,000,000
	=
Number of times each of us could get a spa makeover	8.33

And suddenly, for a few years at least, we're the prettiest nation on earth.

treatments, a thirty-minute massage, warm oil sugar glow (I don't know what that is, but it sure sounds sexy), shampoo, blow dry, makeup application, hydrotherapy Tahitian milk bath, manicure, and spa lunch.

It's 6.5 hours of total pampering, and you emerge looking just like Annette Bening. Okay, maybe not. But maybe you look a bit more like her than you do now.

Now, let's assume that 80 percent of us could benefit from a makeover (exempting children and freaks like Halle Berry who are genetically incapable of looking anything but perfect). We can all afford to get a makeover every year for the next eight years.

There's no way to prove it, but I suspect that we'd all feel better, smile more, and almost certainly have more sex. Which itself would lead to feeling better and smiling more. Which would make us more attractive. Which would lead to more . . . well, you get the idea.

- 31 -

BEST DRESSED
COUNTRY ON EARTH

Gee, America, You Sure Look Purdy

Doesn't it feel good when you look your best? Brand-new clothes, maybe a little more expensive than what you usually buy, shiny new shoes on your feet. Oh, yeah. We need more of that feeling. And we could have it.

No great surprise, I'm sure, to learn that with a trillion dollars to spend, we could all put on some fine new finery.

Ladies, could I interest you in an Armani suit? Of course, it's going to cost you $3,000, and that's just about your entire clothing bonus. The trillion gives us each about $3,300 to spend.

If not the Armani, consider something more casual. Joe's Jeans are pretty hot these days, and only $160 a pair. Buy yourself a few. Oh, and a Juicy Couture track suit—they're the big item in Hollywood these days, you know. Yours for a measly $120. And, since *Sex and the City*, no outfit is complete without a pair of Manolo Blahniks. At $700 or so a pair, I'd recommend at least two pairs. Black and brown, certainly, but maybe something in a fun color, too. And finally, a Chanel handbag for $1,000.

For you, sir, this will be a little more involved. Brace yourself—you're about to spend about ten times what you normally spend in a year on clothes. An Armani suit for you will run about $1,400. (Yes, ladies, it is half the cost of an Armani suit for you, and yes, it is unfair.) Some fine Italian loafers? I think $500 should cover that. And now the great differentiator between those who look good and those who look great—the custom-tailored shirt. At $165 each, you could easily afford half a dozen. Even with all that, you've still got enough left over for a John Edwards haircut.

As for the kids, it's going to be a bit of a challenge to spend $3,300 on kids' clothes. A Juicy Couture outfit is only $120. Joe's Jeans for kids, a trifling $80. For the boys, a Paul Frank

Money spent on Iraq War	$1,000,000,000,000
	÷
Population of USA	303,681,455
	=
Clothing budget for each American	$3,292.92

You're right. It's absurd to spend a trillion dollars on clothes. Especially when so many of us don't even know how to dress. So let's carve a bit off the top for some basic instructions. Ladies—when the space between your buttons puckers, it means your blouse is too tight. Guys—invite your pants down to meet your shoes. By which I mean a longer inseam, not pushing the waist of your pants halfway down your butt.

hoodie and pants for $120, and maybe some Pumas for $74. Buy them a second set of everything in the next larger size (they grow so fast!).

And there's a ton of money left.

Mom, I think you should take another look at those Manolo Blahniks.

- 32 -

THANKING OUR SENIORS

New Buicks All Around

Stereotypes are wrong. Except when they're right.

And when it strikes you that old folks seem to go for Buicks, you're absolutely right. The average age of a Buick owner is sixty-five.

You know what else is true about people who are sixty-five? They built the country you're living in. Everything we enjoy (and too often take for granted) about living in America is built on the foundation that they laid for us.

So this thought is all about a great big "Thank you."

Seniors like Buicks. We owe them. So let's buy them each a new car. With a trillion dollars, we could buy every American over sixty-five a brand-new Buick LaCrosse CX, and still have more than a hundred billion dollars to play with.[128]

But not everyone over sixty-five still drives. One in seven doesn't have a driver's license.[129] So we'd only have to buy cars for about 29 million seniors. Which could mean a much nicer Buick for those who get them.

While the base model LaCrosse costs $23,100,[130] if you step up to a fully loaded Lucerne you're looking at $38,320.[131] Okay, that's not fully loaded. I skipped the navigation system, because

Number of seniors who still drive	29,000,000
	X
Cost of new Buick Lucerne with options for days (including an E85 ethanol conversion kit, to reduce the carbon footprint)	$38,320
	=
Total cost (if we pay sticker price)	$1,111,280,000,000

True, that kind of sweet ride for 29 million seniors would put us overbudget. My hope is that the good folks at GM might cut us a deal if we ordered 29 million cars. Fleets get deals, right? I mean, even if you went into a dealership, you might save enough to make this work. But who wants to hear "What's it gonna take to put you in that car today?" 29 million times?

I figured that adding more technology, and something else to look at, might not be all that helpful for older drivers.

That price does include heated seats, lumbar support, remote vehicle starter system, heated washer fluid, rear parking assist, sunroof, chrome eighteen-inch wheels, and a premium sound system. Seriously, you get the Glenn Miller blasting out of this puppy, it's a party on wheels.

Now consider the side benefits. American auto industry in trouble? Not anymore, my friend. GM sales worldwide in the first quarter of 2007 were 2.26 million vehicles,[132] which might lead you to expect about 10 million vehicles sold through the entire year. Let's push that closer to 40 million next year. Yo, Toyota—who's the big dog now?

Auto workers getting laid off? Flip that on its head. Suddenly, anyone with a pulse could get a job at GM. To say nothing of the people needed to build plants, make tools, sew coveralls, work in the plant cafeterias, truck vehicles across the country, make the signage, do the landscaping around the plant, supply parts, etc., etc. Suddenly, the U.S. economy's on fire.

- 33 -

A WORLD OF MUSIC FESTIVALS

The Future Has a Great Beat and You Can Dance to It

How much could we rock the world for a trillion bucks? Sure, we could buy everybody an iPod, but let's look at it from a different perspective. After all, nothing beats the live music experience.

So how about free music festivals around the planet?

One big lolla-bonna-warped-Ozzy-aroo of a summer. We could even mix up the acts, so people in different parts of the world could experience music from some other region of the planet.

As a model for our world of music festivals, let's use the City Stages Festival in Birmingham, Alabama. Maybe not as big as Bonnaroo, but certainly a well-regarded event. The *Chicago Sun-Times* called it "The best festival you've never heard of." *The Atlanta Journal-Constitution* said it's "the best such event this side of the New Orleans Jazz & Heritage Festival."

For 2007, City Stages had 125 acts playing on nine stages over three days, and drew about 100,000 people. Acts included Bruce Cockburn, Dr. John, Earth Wind & Fire, Ludacris, Ratt, Rickie Lee Jones, Ricky Scaggs, Steve Miller, and a ton of others. Lots of variety, lots of fun.

The budget to stage such an event? Something in the neighborhood of $2.5 million.[133]

That means that with a trillion dollars, we could cover the cost of 400,000 music festivals. Dancing in the streets, indeed.

But isn't that rather a silly and pointless use of a trillion dollars? Would it lead to anything more than millions of people having a good time?

Yes. Potentially a lot. According to independent studies by the Greater Birmingham Convention and Visitors Bureau, City

Money spent on Iraq War	$1,000,000,000,000
	÷
Cost to stage 3-day City Stages Festival	$2,500,000
	=
Number of festivals we could hold	400,000

City Stages has acts that range from bluegrass to hip-hop, but we can go them one better. We'll take American performers around the world, and bring acts from all over the world here. It might just bring us all a little closer together. (Though I confess that when the Chinese music is playing, I'm heading for the concession stands.)

Stages pumps between $10 and $20 million annually into the area economy.[134] Variations on that same story come from virtually all festivals. The total economic impact on Coffee County of the Bonnaroo Music & Arts Festival 2005 was estimated to be $14,087,231 in business revenues, $4,353,887 in personal income, and 191 new jobs.[135] The Austin City Limits Festival contributes $20 million to the economy of the Austin area.[136] And this is not only, or even primarily, an American phenomenon. According to the Swiss office of consultants KPMG, economic activity generated by Hungary's Sziget Festival will reach $54 million by 2010, with much of that going to local businesses, such as hotels and taxi services.[137]

So every city and town in which we hold a festival is liable to see tremendous economic benefits.

Now let's talk about the real money: corporate sponsorship. We could attract the biggest companies in the world, generate billions in sponsorship fees, maybe tens of billions or hundreds of billions—there's really no precedent here, so it's hard to even guess at what we might get. But it's bound to be enough to boggle the mind. And what shall we do with that money? I don't know. After coming up with fifty ways to spend a trillion, I'm kind of, well, spent.

- 34 -

LET'S GO TO
THE MOVIES

Again and Again and Again!

We're stressed out. We don't have enough fun in our lives. We don't spend enough time together as families. We're too cocooned in our homes. We're a fragmented nation, without a shared culture.

There are a world of ills we could cure by just going to the movies more often. Relax, take the night off. Take the kids. Get out of the house. Have something to talk to your coworkers about tomorrow.

Let's use the trillion dollars to go to the movies.

Good news—despite the egregious thievery of popcorn prices at the theater, I'm going to suggest that we could all go to the show once a month. Forever. Courtesy of Uncle Sam.

The National Association of Theatre Owners claims that the average price of a movie ticket in America is $6.55. Which may be true, if you're including second-run theaters, matinees, and every two-dollar-Tuesday or other discount in movie history. In my experience, it's a safer bet to say that going to a movie will cost you 8 or 9 bucks. Plus the aforementioned popcorn. And a drink, 'cuz the popcorn's way too salty. Plus some Twizzlers or Mike and Ikes, 'cuz there are so many trailers and commercials that you go through the popcorn before the movie even starts. Plus parking, 'cuz not many of us live within walking distance of a mondo-plex.

Call it 20 bucks.

As the math shows, if every American went to a movie once a month, it would cost us $72,883,549,200 per year.

Which is less than we could earn in the stock market, according to the Ibbotson forecast of 9 percent annual returns, if we invested the trillion dollars.

Let's use some of the money left over (a bit over $17 billion a year) to invest in America's film business, just to make sure we've got something to watch besides *Halloween 17* and *Rush Hour 9*. (The preceding should not in any way be taken as a knock on Jackie Chan, whose movies my wife and I have a particular fondness for. Can't get enough of 'em.)

Let's build new film schools. Let's bankroll independent films. Let's ban Joan Rivers and her family from the Oscars. No, wait—that's a whole different rant. Let's give Turner Classic Movies a couple of billion dollars, just because it's so cool of them to run classic movies without commercials.

Keep in mind that the movie business is not just entertainment. It provides lots of skilled jobs, pays lots of taxes, and exports America's culture around the world.

Invest $1 trillion in the stock market	$1,000,000,000,000
	X
Growth per year (Ibbotson forecast)	9%
	=
Annual investment income	$90,000,000,000
U.S. population	303,681,455
	X
Cost for movie night	$20
	=
Subtotal	$6,073,629,100
	X
One movie a month	12
	=
Total annual cost	$72,883,549,200

Next question—is there anything at the multiplex worth seeing?

The last point may be the most important of all. If we really want the world to be more like the USA, maybe invading them and wreaking havoc is not as effective as entertaining them and warping their minds (in a good way, of course). A generation that grows up idolizing Will Ferrell or falling in love with Mathew Mc-Conaughey or Angelina Jolie might want to be more like them. And aren't most American movies morality plays, in one way or another? The good guys win. The true-blue guy gets the girl. Truth and honor and decency virtually always come out on top.

Ironic, when you consider the sort of people who run the movie business, but true nonetheless.

So with this plan, we all go to the movies a lot, enjoy evenings with friends and family, support an important American industry (take that, Bollywood!), and subject the rest of the world to even more propaganda than ever before.

Sounds like a happy ending to me.

- 35 -

VACATIONS FOR ALL

I'm Going to Disneyland!
And the Government's Paying for It!

An AP-Ipsos poll last year found that only half of Americans were planning a summer vacation, but that 79 percent would take one if they could afford it and had the time.[138] You'll have to solve the time crunch for yourself, but with a trillion dollars, we could all afford to go just about anywhere we want to.

Turns out, for a lot of us, that would mean a Disney vacation. A Zagat survey found that five of the eight most popular attractions in America are Disney resorts.[139] (In the interest of full disclosure, it should be noted that Hyperion, the company that published this book, is a part of Disney. The author, though, has never been to a Disney park and is no way recommending them for vacations. However, should Hyperion wish to send the author to Disneyland, he would be more than happy to go and to subsequently enthusiastically endorse the parks to anyone he meets. In a completely professional, objective way, of course.)

Fodor's estimates the average cost of a vacation at a Disney resort for a family of four to be about $500 per day including hotel, food, and tickets.[140] A pittance, when each person's share of the trillion dollars would come to about $3,300 in vacation money to spend. In fact, that trillion dollars could pay for your family's summer vacation this year, and next year, and the year after that, and leave almost enough left over to pay for a fourth year.

The picture changes a little if your dream is to see Rome or Rio. YPB&R/Yankelovich (a leading market research firm) estimates that the average vacation in the USA costs about $1,000, and the average international vacation costs about $3,500.[141]

As for finding the time for a vacation, some of us have to get better at that. Studies have shown that half of American workers take only half the vacation time they're entitled to. Joe Robinson, author of *Work to Live: The Guide to Getting a Life*,

Cost of a week at Disneyland for each person in a family of four	$875
	X
People in the USA	303,681,455
	=
Total cost	$265,721,273,125

So everybody in America gets an all-expenses-paid trip to Disneyland and we've barely spent a quarter of the money. We could each get three more free vacations. How about Epcot, Magic Kingdom, and then Animal Kingdom? Or, if you insist, someplace that's not owned by Disney. Though that seems vaguely un-American, if you ask me.

says, "Time off is medicine. It's as important to your health as watching your cholesterol or getting exercise. An annual vacation can cut the risk of heart disease in men by 30 percent and in women by 50 percent."

Vacations—they're fun, they're good for you, and with a trillion dollars to split among us, they'd be virtually free.

- 36 -

DREAMS COME TRUE

Yours, Mine, Everybody's

Somewhere in the back of your grown-up mind there's a childhood dream. To be a cowboy, to drive a race car, to be a rock star, to climb a mountain. Or maybe you have grown-up dreams of great meals and fine wines in Italy or romantic nights in Paris.

To no one's great surprise, a trillion dollars can make a lot of dreams come true.

As we boomers have "grown up," entire industries have grown alongside us to feed our fantasies. If you've dreamed of playing tennis with Chris Evert, boxing with Sugar Ray Leonard, or shooting hoops with James Worthy, now you can do it.

Perhaps the greatest of the fantasy businesses is Rock 'n' Roll Fantasy Camp. You can jam with Roger Daltrey, Bill Wyman, Brian Wilson, Spencer Davis, Steve Vai, Levon Helm, Paul Stanley, and dozens of other certified rock stars. For a little less glamour and a little more learning, you could spend a week at Fur Peace Ranch with Jorma Kaukonen and Jack Casady (of Jefferson Airplane and Hot Tuna).

Or, you could, if you hadn't spent all that money on the war.

Actually, not all of us can attend the biggest of the adult "live the dream" vacations. Rock 'n' Roll Fantasy Camp and Ultimate

Money spent on Iraq War	$1,000,000,000,000
	÷
Americans between 18 and 75 years old (kids can still become real rock stars if they want, and I'm assuming that most seventy-five-year-olds don't want to go to rodeo camp)	204,790,000[142]
	=
Amount you can spend on your fantasy vacation	$4,883

Go ahead—spend a minute thinking about your unfulfilled dream. The book will still be here when you get back.

Sports Fantasy Camp carry price tags from $6,000 up to $30,000, depending on the package you choose. And even with a trillion dollars, we can't afford to send everyone on these ultimate fantasy vacations.

At the other end of the scale, though, there's Pro Wrestling Fantasy Camp for just $1,000. Richard Petty's race driving school can have you driving on the track at Daytona, Bristol, Talladega, or the Indianapolis Speedway for as little as $399. And adventure holidays like diving in the Great Barrier Reef also cost less than hanging with Slash and Joe Walsh (though the parties may not be as good).

So here's the deal: as long as enough of us prefer climbing the Matterhorn or doing the *City Slickers* thing and playing cowboy (sorry, Jack Palance not included), then we could average out the cost so that every American adult's dream could come true.

I'll tell you mine if you tell me yours.

- 37 -

WORLD'S FAIRS
ACROSS AMERICA

The World at Your Doorstep

Americans are often accused of not knowing much about the rest of the world. And, truth be told, most of us are guilty.

It doesn't help that the mainstream media in this country tend to ignore the rest of the planet. Let's face it, if Americans aren't killing or being killed, we really don't hear or see that much of anything beyond our borders.

Maybe if we all knew a little bit more about the rest of the world, we wouldn't do so many things that seem to piss them off. (Not that it's all our fault. Most of them—especially the French—are way too sensitive. And would it be so hard for them to learn English?)

One great way to learn about other countries is by visiting a world's fair. Problem is, they only come along every five years, and as often as not, they're half a world away. So let's hold a world's fair. In fact, let's hold fifty of them—one in every state. (It's nice to see the world, but it would be even better if you didn't have to travel so much, right?)

The last big world's fair was in Aichi Prefecture, Japan (just east of Nagoya) (which is southwest of Tokyo) (which is sort of in the middle of Japan). Cost of the fair was estimated at $3.3 billion.[143] Of course, in a real world's fair, most countries pay to build their own pavilions. Pretty doubtful that we could get them to pony up for fifty pavilions across America, so we'll pay for them ourselves. Wild ballpark here, but let's say that drives the cost to stage a fair up to $10 billion.

We'll hire architects from each country to reflect their design heritage. Bring in chefs from each country so we can try their food. Bring in bands so we can hear their music. Show films and videos. Sell their fashions and handicrafts in the gift shops.

Money spent on Iraq War	$1,000,000,000,000
	—
Cost of world's fair X 50	$500,000,000,000
	=
Money left over	$500,000,000,000

What to do with the other $500 billion? Here's a thought. Off the coast of Dubai, they're creating islands in the shape of a map of the world. The project is costing $14 billion. We could build the world in each of America's thirty-six largest lakes. You could buy Ireland or Australia and build yourself a little cottage. Or buy Iraq and put up a big American flag.

And throw in a few roller coasters and a water park, just to make sure we attract big crowds.

Bring the kids. Have a world of fun.

- 38 -

A GENERATION OF COLLEGE SCHOLARSHIPS

Smarten Up, America

What if everyone in America had a college degree? The money being spent on the war is enough to provide every American child who's currently in high school with a free four-year university education—even if none of them play football.

Suddenly, America becomes the most well-educated nation on earth. That just might help us be competitive in a global

Number of Americans in high school	16,724,086
	X
Cost of 4 years' tuition and fees (average of public and private colleges)[144]	$59,794
	=
Total cost	$999,999,998,284

We have $1,716 left over. Maybe just enough to host a press conference to let everyone know the good news.

economy. And what would it mean to teenagers in low-income neighborhoods to know that they can go to college and have a real shot at a future? Might it convince some of them to stay away from drugs and criminal behavior? Might we see fewer teenage pregnancies? If optimism replaced hopelessness in our inner cities, how many lives might change for the better?

Beyond that, we'd have almost 17 million[145] people starting their working lives without college loans hanging over their heads. That would have a lasting effect on their financial lives.

We'd also have millions of parents who could be saving for retirement, paying down their mortgages, or buying sports cars instead of paying for their kids to go to college.

- 39 -

SMALLER CLASSES, SMARTER KIDS

And How About a Raise for Teachers?

I'm not the smartest person in the world, but it seems to me that if America wants to be the number one country in the world in years to come, we should have the smartest kids in the world right now.

And we don't.

In the most recent international mathematics competition, American eighth graders ranked nineteenth out of thirty-eight countries that participated. In a 1995 international assessment of math and science literacy, the USA ranked eighteenth out of twenty-one countries tested. For those who struggle with numbers, let me assure you, that's not good.[146]

We're not much better when it comes to language. In the most recent Program for International Student Assessment combined reading literacy scale tests, American fifteen-year-olds scored about average. Canadian, Finnish, and New Zealand students had the highest scores.[147]

That makes us, overall, somewhere between average and total losers—that's just unAmerican, isn't it? Could a trillion dollars help set things right?

Let's assume that America's kids aren't genetically predisposed to being stupid. Let's go a step further and be daring enough to suggest that American kids are as smart as Canadians or Finns, or anybody else for that matter.

If our kids are starting with as much potential as other kids, maybe it's on us to do more to develop that potential. A great many people, including teachers, suggest that the best way to do that is to reduce class size. A number of studies have been done to prove the point.

Invest $1 trillion in the stock market	$1,000,000,000,000
	X
Growth per year (Ibottson forecast)	9%
	=
Total to be dispersed each year	$90,000,000,000
	÷
Average teacher salary	$46,597
	=
Number of new teachers	1,931,455

This takes average class size down to about fourteen kids. Maybe they don't have to get quite that small. If we don't hire so many teachers, we could afford to give all teachers a raise. Given that their salary is roughly on par with a legal secretary or a convenience store manager, I don't think that would be out of line.

According to the most recent Department of Education statistics, the average class size across America is 21.1 for public elementary schools and 23.6 for public secondary schools.[148] Studies have generally shown that getting class size below 20 students is a turning point.

So let's do that. In fact, in the grandest of American traditions, let's overdo it.

Take the trillion dollars and invest it in the stock market. As in other chapters, we'll use the Ibbotson forecast of 9 percent growth per year. So even if we never touch the principal, we should get about $90 billion a year to play with. Which means we could hire 1,931,455 additional teachers. (I know the math gets a bit heady here for those who went to American schools, but trust me.)

There are currently just over 3 million teachers in America, so with the new hires, we'd have about 5 million teachers nationwide. Allowing for the fact that some teachers are involved in work other than standing in front of a class, that would cut class size to perhaps 14 for both elementary and secondary schools.

We get smaller classes, smarter kids, and a reason to believe that in the future, we'll be academically kicking Finnish butt.

- 40 -

RETRAIN AMERICA'S WORKERS

Does Life After the Factory Have to Include the Phrase "Welcome to Wal-Mart"?

The refrain of the Wal-Mart greeter is often used as a symbol of the ultimate last-ditch job. The irony, of course, being that Wal-Mart's Chinese imports are one of the reasons why American factory workers are out of work in the first place. But that's another book altogether.

The issue here is that since 2000, we've lost 3.2 million factory jobs.[149] Other sectors are hurting, too. Membership in the United Mine Workers is down 80 percent from its peak.[150] Those solid working-class jobs with a good wage, a pension, and benefits are disappearing. The families that depended on them, though, are still among us.

Sadly, that's just the beginning. As broadband networks grow, more and more service and technology work is moving outside our borders. The U.S. Business and Industry Council examined 114 U.S. industries and found that 110 of them had lost ground to imports in the U.S. market.[151] Princeton economist Alan Blinder (former vice chairman of the Federal Reserve) says the number of jobs at risk of being shipped out of the country could reach 40 million over the next ten to twenty years.[152]

As time goes on, more and more of us will have to get used to

Invest $1 trillion in the stock market	$1,000,000,000,000
	X
Growth per year (Ibbotson forecast)	9%
	=
Total to be dispersed each year	$90,000,000,000
Cost per year of community college	$11,692
	X
Americans in the program each year	4,000,000
	=
Total annual cost	$46,768,000,000

The $43 billion left over could be used to help families with their living expenses. Or to invest in new industries to take the place of the industrial-age companies that are fading away.

not just changing jobs, but changing careers. If you don't want to find yourself asking if the customer wants fries with that, you'll want to get some fresh, job-oriented knowledge and skills.

A good place to do that is America's network of 1,150 community colleges. Average tuition cost is only $2,191 a year, though by the time you factor in books and basic living expenses, you can expect to spend $11,692.[153]

Blinder's prediction suggests that, for the next decade or two, we should expect to lose about 2 million jobs a year. Can we afford to send that many Americans back to school?

In a heartbeat. The total cost would be $23,384,000,000. Of course, we'd actually pay double that, since most community college programs are two years long, so we'd be retraining two years' worth of unemployed Americans at any given time. Even then, we'd only spend about half of what we could earn through investing the trillion dollars.

We could even help to cover the lost income of those years so that families don't live in poverty while Mom and/or Dad goes back to school. We couldn't give them the sort of income they probably enjoyed while working in factories or mines. But even if you have to shop at Wal-Mart for a couple of years, it sure beats working there for the rest of your life.

- 41 -

NO SMOKING
ANYWHERE

The Butt Stops Here

Tobacco use is the leading preventable cause of premature death in the United States. Smoking-related health care costs nearly $3.5 billion annually. Yeah, yeah, yeah. We've all heard it all before.

Those who aren't smokers hassle those who are, and most people who are smokers wish they could quit. Most, in fact, have tried. A number of times. And failed.

Believe me (cough), I know how hard it is. When smokers try to quit, they fail between 90 percent and 97 percent of the time. There are, though, a variety of things that can help—from nicotine substitution products to help lines to hypnotherapy to those annoying, accusatory ads on TV. Naturally, all of them cost money.

In the interest of America's 47 million smokers,[154] and the rest of you who get tagged with higher health insurance costs because of us, let's invest some money in breaking this habit.

The Centers for Disease Control and Prevention did a study of various methods to help smokers quit, looking at their cost and effectiveness.[155] Let's embrace every approach that's demonstrated proven effectiveness. Based on the CDC's records of what's worked in the past, we could reasonably expect to see 6 million Americans quit smoking in the first year.

	Cost per Quitter[156]	Percentage Who Quit
Media campaign	$1,593	2
	+	+
Financial support for cessation materials (e.g., "We'll help you pay for the Patch")	$195	8
	+	+
Support lines	$1,248	3
	=	=
Total cost	$3,036	13
	X	
47,000,000 smokers	$142,692,000,000	6,110,000 quitters

The good news is, this would alleviate some of the health care issues we discussed in earlier chapters. The bad news is that the quitters would live longer, so the Social Security problems would get even worse.

Since many smokers, even with help, need to try to quit a number of times before they ultimately succeed, we'll repeat the program year after year. The cost would actually go down each year, as we'll have fewer smokers to help, but to keep the budgeting simple, let's assume the same cost every year.

By year four of the effort, we'd have spent just over half our trillion ($570,768,000,000) and we'd have half the number of smokers in America that we have today.

And be breathing a lot easier.

- 42 -

BRINGING WATERWAYS BACK TO LIFE

Los Angeles Has a River? Really?

Perhaps no river in America has been more abused than the Los Angeles River. You probably know it as that huge concrete ditch in *Chinatown, Terminator 2*, and other movies. Yes, that's actually a river.

What's exciting is that it seems to be on its way to becoming a real river again. With vegetation and fish, and grass and trees alongside of it. And it's beginning to play the critical role that rivers play in the ecosystem.

Plans for the river include a series of parks (called the Greenway Project) woven together by biking and walking paths to stretch from the San Fernando Valley to Long Beach, which will serve as both green space and flood control mechanisms. Regulations now require municipalities to reduce trash by 10 percent each year. Los Angeles has even increased spending on street sweeping, trash pickup, and education on water cleanliness.

None of this comes cheap. Buying land for park space, better water treatment facilities, preventing street waste from entering the river—it all costs money. About $1.5 billion has been pledged by various groups and governments to make it happen in Los Angeles.[157] But if it can happen there, it can happen anywhere.

And in fact, it *is* happening. St. Louis, Providence, and Boston are all making progress on their rivers.

On the flip side, a study by the National River Restoration Science Synthesis revealed that from about 1973 to 1998, rivers and lakes in the United States were getting cleaner, but that's now reversed itself. More than a third of U.S. rivers are listed as polluted or impaired. Extinction rates of freshwater fish are about five times the level of land animals. So there's a lot of work to be done.

Have no fear, though. We've got a trillion dollars we can use

Money spent on Iraq War	$1,000,000,000,000
	÷
Cost to restore (at least partially) the Los Angeles River to health	$1,500,000,000
	=
Number of rivers that could be cleaned up and revitalized	667

Given that American Rivers, a river conservation organization, called the Los Angeles River the most endangered urban waterway in the country, it's probably fair to assume that we could actually help a lot more rivers than that.

to set this right. Since life without water would be, well, impossible, it's hard to imagine what could be a more important use for the money.

- 43 -

MASS MASS-TRANSIT

Parking's a Hassle, Let's Take the Monorail

How much cleaner would the air be if every major city in America had a great mass-transit system? How much might that free us from our dependence on foreign oil? How much would it cost?

First, we need to accept that bus lines won't do it. Every city in America has buses, and just about all of us will choose our own car over a bus every time. Build a subway or a light rail system with trains coming every few minutes, and you've changed the game.

Most cities don't do it because of the enormous capital cost, particularly of subways. Las Vegas recently built a monorail system. It's four miles long, with seven stations. Different sources quote different costs, from $87 million per mile[158] to $100 million per mile,[159] even up to $148 million per mile.[160]

In Los Angeles, a monorail plan is being floated for the Wilshire corridor, and being quoted at $141 million per mile.[161]

If we're going to think about monorails for other cities, let's be extra prudent, and estimate on the high end—call it $150 million per mile. With a trillion dollars to spend, we could cover about 6,667 miles of rail service.

That's roughly the distance from New York to Tokyo. While a New York–to-Tokyo monorail is kind of a cool idea, it may not be the most practical way to use the money.

Instead, let's put 66 miles of monorail in each of America's 100 largest cities. That would dwarf even some of the larger rail systems that currently exist. Dallas's DART runs 40 miles. Portland's system covers 38.5 miles. Pittsburgh's T runs for 25 miles. And people love them. In each case, ridership is running well ahead of projections. Presently, Dallas averages 38,000 riders on weekdays, Portland 27,000, and Pittsburgh 80,000. Their numbers are not atypical for major cities across the nation.

Money spent on Iraq War	$1,000,000,000,000
	÷
Cost per mile for monorail	$150,000,000
	=
Miles of monorail system we could build	6,667

Urban rail systems seem to generate about 1,000 passengers per mile of system on each weekday. Which suggests that with as much monorail construction as we're proposing above, we could get about 7 million commuters off our roads. That might even make rush hour in Atlanta bearable.

Now dramatically increase the size of those systems. Build monorails in cities that don't currently have good transit. Over 100 cities, how many cars would we take off the roads every day? How much less oil would we consume? How much less would we pollute the air?

Could we postpone or eliminate new highway construction? Extend the life of our vehicles by driving them less? Reduce the number of traffic accidents? Eliminate road rage?

Questions to contemplate when you drive to work tomorrow.

- 44 -

AN EXERCISE IN, WELL, EXERCISE

The USA, aka Fat, Fat the Water Rat

This is a big country. And, sadly, getting bigger every day. We're packing on pounds at a dangerous rate, and a report in the journal *Epidemiologic Review* suggests that in less than ten years, 75 percent of the population will be overweight, and 41 percent will be obese.[162] Dr. John Foreyt at the Baylor College of Medicine in Houston has gone so far as to predict that "100 percent of the population will be overweight or obese by 2040."[163]

Which doesn't bode well for either the NBA or the Miss America pageant. But I digress.

It's easy to say that this is happening because we sit on the couch and eat chips while watching sports instead of, say, getting up and playing sports. That's not universally true—there are people with inescapable genetic issues. But for most of us, this is happening because we sit on the couch and eat chips while watching sports instead of, say, getting up and playing sports.

And this is about more than just how we look. Heart disease, diabetes, even some cancers can stem from weight issues.[164]

According to *The Surgeon General's Call to Action to Prevent and Decrease Overweight and Obesity,* the cost of obesity in the United States in 2000 was more than $117 billion.[165] That, of course, was eight years and a few thousand tons ago, so the cost is probably a lot higher now.

So whaddya say we invest the trillion dollars in becoming a lean, mean, national machine?

With that kind of money, we could each have a personal trainer to guide and motivate us. We could all join a gym, or we could have a home gym in every home. A ThighMaster for every

Cost of Bowflex Blaze home gym	$899
	+
ThighMaster	$20
	+
Reebok Vista Treadmill (with built-in TV!)	$1,199
	+
Nike Air Zoom shoes (average 3 pairs per household)	$360
	+
iPod nano and Nike + iPod Sport Kit (3 sets)	$684
	+
Personal trainer (12 sessions)	$600
	=
Total per household	$3,762
	X
Number of households in USA	112,362,848[166]
	=
Total cost	$422,709,034,176

We've spent less than half the money, and damn, America, you look hot!

thigh. A treadmill in every house, apartment, condo, and work-place in the country. And everybody gets one of those cool Nike + iPod systems to make walking or running a rock-and-roll party.

We'd look better, feel better, have more energy, live longer, and save billions on health care. From where I sit (on the couch, watching football), that sounds like a heck of a plan.

- 45 -

MEDICAL RESEARCH
Whaddya Say We Cure Cancer?

Putting a trillion dollars into medical research is an intriguing thought. It could deliver longer lives for most of us and a better quality of life for all of us. The economic benefits are potentially massive, too. Medical research is an industry that provides high-income jobs, both directly, and indirectly with its need for high technology. Plus, better health means increased productivity for American workers. Advances in medicine could reduce the health care costs that threaten to cripple our economy as the population ages.

But hard numbers and specific proof points just aren't possible. We are, by definition, stepping into uncharted territory.

In spite of that, most Americans recognize the value of medical research. In a 2005 poll, most Americans (55 percent) said they'd go along with higher taxes to fund more medical research.[167]

Maybe because we've seen what it can do for us. Polio and smallpox are virtually historical footnotes now. We've seen a 50 to 60 percent increase in six-year cancer survival rates since 1975.[168] Death rates from heart disease fell by 40 percent between 1975 and 2000. For stroke victims, the death rate fell 51 percent. The number of AIDS-related deaths fell by about 70 percent between 1995 and 2001.[169]

Maybe we support the idea because the Congressional Budget Office estimates that by 2050, the combined cost of Medicare and Medicaid alone will consume a larger share of the nation's income *than the entire federal budget does today*.

But is there reason to believe that a trillion dollars could have a real effect on our collective health in the future? It would certainly be a sizeable boost from current levels of spending, which run about $100 billion.[170]

Well, here's where it gets really exciting. To this point in history, medical research has been largely focused on chemistry. We are now at the dawn of a new era. "In the new age we are now entering, we will increasingly use advanced biology to actually cure or even prevent disease from occurring," according to Sidney Taurel, president and CEO of Eli Lilly and Company.[171]

So we find ourselves on the brink of a whole new field of study—one that goes to a deep understanding of how the body forms, operates, and mutates. And through the exponential growth in technology, we have tools beyond anything we've ever known.

Invest $1 trillion in the stock market	$1,000,000,000,000
	X
Growth per year (Ibbotson forecast)	9%
	=
Total to be dispersed each year	$90,000,000,000
	+
Current spending on medical research	$100,000,000,000
	=
New total spending on research	$190,000,000,000

It costs an average of $802 million to get one new medicine from the laboratory to U.S. patients, so we've just funded 112 new medicines.[172] Mind you, the process takes ten to fifteen years, so we'd better get started.[173]

What a great time to increase funding. Let's invest the trillion dollars and use the earnings on it to fund research. We
could almost double the research that we currently do.

I feel better already.

- 46 -

THE WONDERS OF
THE WORLD

Turn Left at the Pyramid; If You See
Versailles Palace, You've Gone Too Far

Now that the rest of the world has renewed their love affair
with anti-Americanism, traveling the globe can be a problem. So let's bring the best of the world here.

Let's re-create all the wonders of the world, right here in the
USA. New York can have a pyramid. How about some Easter Is-
land statues on the hills around L.A.? Boston can have its own
Guggenheim Museum Bilbao. Phoenix gets the Sydney Opera
House. The Taj Mahal might look good near the lake in Chicago.
Stonehenge for Atlanta. Nashville loves the Greek stuff—let's give
them a real Acropolis.

Sure, it's hard to figure exact costs for this. Even if you knew
the cost of the original Acropolis, how do you calculate the effects of inflation over 2,500 years? The most recent of these
buildings, Frank Gehry's Guggenheim Museum in Bilbao, cost
$100,000,000 to build.[174] If we take that as an average, it would
surely mean that we'd run out of wonders to build long before
we ran out of money.

To spend all the money, we'd have to build a Wonder of the
World in 10,000 American cities and towns. Which means we'd
be building in some pretty small towns. Nothing wrong with
that, of course, although they might get a building that's not all

Money spent on Iraq War	$1,000,000,000,000
	÷
Cost of Guggenheim Museum Bilbao	$100,000,000
	=
Cities that get a "Wonder"	10,000

What a great time to be in the construction trades! Plus, being surrounded by great buildings is uplifting and inspirational. This could stimulate a great new age of creativity in America.

that special anyhow, because really, what's the 10,000th most wonderful building on earth? And do we really need to provoke a fight between Hungry Horse, Montana, and Burnt Corn, Alabama, over who does and doesn't get a building?

Maybe we should just give a few hundred billion to America's best architects and see what they can come up with that's brand-new.

"Hello, Mr. Gehry?"

- 47 -

PAVE THE STREETS WITH GOLD

Yes, We Actually Could

Clearly this is the most absurd idea in the book. Though one might still argue that it makes more sense than invading Iraq.

Imagine waking up in the morning to find the entire nation bathed in warm, glowing, golden light. Imagine the reaction of a first-time visitor to the USA—sitting in the back of a cab, a little jet-lagged, heading from the airport to downtown with mouth hanging open in shock and awe. "In America," they will tell the disbelievers back home, "the streets are paved with gold."

A trillion dollars, of course, doesn't buy what it used to. So we're not talking about cobblestones of gold ingots. More like gold leaf over the existing asphalt. But 23.5-karat gold leaf, not some sort of cheap imitation.

And we could cover every highway in the land.

The U.S. Department of Transportation (who should know) tells us that there are 280,264 miles of highway in this great land.[175] That includes interstates, principal and minor arterial highways, collectors, and local highways. A pretty exhaustive list. And we could cover every inch of all those highways in gold.

Take those 280,264 miles of highway. Assume that, on average, they're four lanes wide. According to motorists.org, the recommended width for a lane is twelve feet. Convert miles to feet and feet to inches, you end up with 10,228,335,575,000 square inches of highway to be resurfaced.

A sheet of gold leaf, for those who haven't bought any re-

Money spent on Iraq War	$1,000,000,000,000
	−
Cost to pave every highway in the USA in gold	$355,033,135,661.40
	=
Money remaining to pave the streets of our cities	$644,966,864,338.60

True, the gold leaf would wear off pretty quickly. But it would surely be a sight that none of us would ever forget. We'd probably all have that look that children and puppies get the first time they see a snowfall. And I guarantee that each and every one of us would tell our grandchildren about the days when the streets were paved with gold.

cently, is 30.25 square inches, so it would take 338,126,795,868 sheets of gold leaf to cover every highway in America.

Each sheet costs $1.05. And that's shopping retail.[176]

Which brings us to a total cost of $355,033,135,661.40. A lot of money, but only a fraction of our trillion dollars.

Now, with just under $650 billion left, let's turn our attention to the roads of our cities and towns. Start with New York City as a model. There are 6,200 miles of roadway in the Big Apple.[177] Most cities will have a lot less than that, of course, but we're also assuming two-lane roads for this exercise, and some city streets will be wider than that.

If those assumptions balance each other out, then our leftover money could pave the streets of every city in America with a population greater than 150,000—about 160 municipalities in all.[178] And there would probably be enough left over to ensure that every town and village in the country could, at the very least, have their Main Street paved in gold. Which could make for some pretty dazzling parades come the Fourth of July.

- 48 -

PAY CRIMINALS TO BEHAVE

Will Bad Guys Be Good If You Pay Them?

What state has a bigger population than Alaska, Delaware, DC, Hawaii, Idaho, Maine, Montana, Nebraska, New Hampshire, New Mexico, North Dakota, Rhode Island, South Dakota, Vermont, West Virginia, or Wyoming?

The state of incarceration.

According to the U.S. Bureau of Justice Statistics, the population of the nation's prisons and jails rose to a new record last year. Some 2.26 million of us are now living in lockup.[179] That's one in every 134 Americans. Some of them, to be sure, are bad, bad people. They deserve to be put in a bad, bad place and we all sleep better at night knowing that there are bars and fences and armed guards between those bad people and us.

But we incarcerate more people than any other nation in the world. The USA has 5 percent of the world's population, but 25 percent of the world's prison population.[180] Maybe there's a better way to deal with some of those people. Especially since a lot of them are not violent criminals. In fact, now 60 percent of federal inmates are drug offenders,[181] who on average receive longer sentences than violent felons do.[182]

Sure, people who break the law should pay a penalty. Let's

Invest $1 trillion in the stock market	$1,000,000,000,000
	X
Growth per year (Ibbotson forecast)	9%
	=
Funds available each year	$90,000,000,000
	÷
Prisoners released with good-behavior reward plan	1,356,000
	=
Amount available annually for each former prisoner	$66,371.68

Of course, we're not talking about giving them nearly that much money. If we go with $20,000 per year, we'd only spend $27,120,000,000. Leaving almost $63 billion a year for programs to help keep people off drugs and out of prison in the first place. And we wouldn't be spending the $22,000 each year that it costs us to keep each of them in prison.

Hang on—$22,000 a year to keep them inside? Oh, man, that's less than it costs to keep them behaving on the outside. Turns out we don't even need to touch the trillion.

focus for the moment, though, more on ensuring that they don't break the law again.

Forget about the violent ones. Leave them behind bars, thank you very much. And I mean that—thank you very much for keeping those people behind bars. Look at the 60 percent who are drug offenders—potentially 1,356,000 prisoners nationwide.

With a trillion dollars, we could give each of them $737,463.13, if they promise to behave themselves. Not all at once, of course. Give three-quarters of a million dollars each to more than a million people with a history of drug use and all you'll get is the biggest party America's ever seen.

I'm suggesting that we make them serve a year in the pen, so we can all feel like they've been punished. After that, we offer a reward of maybe $20,000 at the end of each year in which they've managed to stay clean and out of trouble. Even if they each live for another forty or fifty years, we'd be covered with even a minimal amount of interest on our trillion.

It could reunite families, turn prisoners into productive citizens, inject money into the economy, and save some of the billions of dollars we're now spending to build new prisons. I know—crazy idea.

- 49 -

THE GREENING
OF OUR CITIES

Park It Right Here

If there's a city in America that suffers from too many parks, I've never been there. But there are plenty of places where you can go for blocks and blocks without a tree, a flower, or a blade of grass in sight.

That's not good, on all kinds of levels. Whatever a park might mean to you—a place to take your kids, a quiet spot to eat your lunch, a place where trees and grass can pump oxygen back into the urban air, or just a visual break from the concrete—I suspect that most of us would agree that a few more parks would make our cities a little more livable.

So let's buy up some land and build nothing on it. Well, maybe a swing set and a few benches.

It won't be cheap. Land, especially in urban areas, gets more expensive with each passing year. In New York City, for example, the land for the Hudson Yards development has been valued as high as $50 million per acre.[183] (For New Yorkers and other urbanites, an acre is a little larger than 200 feet by 200 feet.) Naturally, other cities are less expensive, but they're still not cheap. A survey of recent land deals across the nation shows Boca Raton, Raleigh, and parts of Los Angeles at about $3 million an acre; Miami can cost you $2 million an acre, and Jacksonville's running

Half of the money spent on Iraq War	$500,000,000,000
	÷
Cost of one acre	$500,000
	=
Acres of land we could buy	1,000,000
Invest half of the money spent on Iraq War	$500,000,000,000
	X
Growth per year (Ibbotson forecast)	9%
	=
Money to spend each year on landscaping/upkeep	$45,000,000,000

The first 18,443 people to get behind me on this one get a park named after them.

at just over $1 million. At the other end of the scale, Jackson County, Michigan, promises land as low as $4,000 per acre.

It's tough to find an average in all of that, but let's set ourselves an arbitrary price of $500,000 per acre, which is probably a fair price for land in midsize cities. And let's not spend the entire trillion, because we should give the cities some money for landscaping and upkeep.

Even at that high price for land, and even if we only spend half of the trillion dollars, we're looking at 1 million acres of new parkland for America's cities. That's equivalent to almost 1,200 Central Parks.

So we could declare that the 1,200 largest cities in America each get a Central Park.

Or, to spread things out a little more, we could decide that every city, town, and village in the nation should get some new parkland. There are, according to the U.S. Census, 18,443 of them. Meaning that every municipality in the nation could get just over 54 acres of new parkland.

- 50 -

GET ADVICE FROM THE EXPERTS

Ask a Hollywood Star

Whether it's Barbra Streisand on international relations or Ed Begley, Jr., on the environment, it should be clear to us all by now that Hollywood stars have all the answers. They've certainly never been shy about offering up their point of view (or POV, as they say in the film scripts).

To be fair, an ability to sing or act or tell jokes shouldn't exempt a person from their right to voice an opinion on politics. The problem is less with them than it is with us. We too often attach an importance to their views far beyond what we'd give our neighbors, family members, or coworkers.

Yet our neighbors, family members, and coworkers almost certainly have a clearer sense of what matters to most Americans. You know, the ones who live in "fly-over" country, clean their own houses, and sweat about car payments. One might argue that Hollywood royalty is out of touch with the needs and beliefs of "regular" Americans. Then again, Kennedys and Bushes don't exactly live "regular" lives, and we've trusted the nation to them more than once.

The right is often quick to mock the Hollywood elite and their political involvement, yet it was the right that brought Ronald Reagan to the White House. In contemporary politics, we have Republican Governor Arnold Schwarzenegger and Republican former senator Fred Thompson. The exceptions in this case seem to prove the rule, though, and clearly the vast majority of La-La-Land activists are firmly planted on the left end of the spectrum.

Which means it may not be possible to get a fair representation of the political spectrum out of Hollywood. That does not, though, mean the exercise is by definition without merit.

So I'm throwing open an invitation to each and every star in Hollywood who's ever offered up a political opinion . . . Rob Reiner, Bradley Whitford, Michelle Pfeiffer, Tom Cruise, Steven Spielberg, Sharon Stone, Cameron Diaz, Angelina Jolie (especially Angelina Jolie), Don Cheadle, Denzel Washington, Sean Penn, Kelsey Grammer, Norman Lear, Jane Fonda, Michael J. Fox, Robert Redford, Warren Beatty, Susan Sarandon, Tim Robbins, Danny Glover, Ed Asner, Adam Sandler, Scarlett Johansson (especially Scarlett Johansson), Meg Ryan, Richard Dreyfuss, Salma Hayek (especially Salma Hayek, too), George Clooney, heck, even Chuck Norris . . . if you've got some thoughts on how we might have spent the trillion dollars, let me know. And if I've left you off the list, my apologies. Please have your publicist get in touch.

Maybe we can even get a second book out of this. Or at least a network special.

Seriously, Salma, call me.

FINALLY . . .

This is a wealthy nation, and we could be doing extraordinary things with our money. When our leaders make poor choices, it's up to us to hold them accountable. To do that, we need to be aware of what they're doing, and also what they're choosing not to do.

Remember that democracy bestows not only rights, but also obligations on its citizens. Be informed. Be involved. Be vocal. Vote.

REGARDING THE NUMBERS

- The trillion-dollar figure used throughout this book comes from, among others, the Congressional Budget Office.[184] Some people, including Columbia University economist Joseph E. Stiglitz (winner of the Nobel Prize in economics in 2001 and former chief economist at the World Bank) now peg the cost at well over $2 trillion,[185] but we've opted to use the official, albeit more conservative number.

- There are a number of places throughout the book where we reference Roger Ibbotson's forecasts of stock market growth to estimate annual income that might have been received had the trillion dollars been broadly invested in American companies. Ibbotson has been widely regarded as America's leading forecaster of market performance for more than thirty years. Market performance over the past twenty-five years might lead one to expect returns of 12 percent per year, but we have generally opted to use more conservative numbers and gone with the Ibbotson forecasts, which call for future growth of 9 percent per year.

- The sources for numbers cited are wide, varied, and obtained through Internet research from Web sites or printed government sources in the public domain. The author has made every effort to ensure the accuracy of the

statistical information presented but cannot ensure complete accuracy of third-party data and as such assumes no
liability in its presentation or redistribution. This information and related statistics should be used as a general
guide for information purposes only.

ACKNOWLEDGMENTS

Rather a ridiculous amount of research has gone into this little book, and I am most grateful to Dave Townsend, Laura Black, Martin Buchanan, Kate Harrow, and Donna Felskie for their assistance. Shout-outs also go to my agent, Rick Broadhead, who was quick to believe in this idea and tireless in advancing the cause; and to my editor, Brendan Duffy, who kept the book on track and made it stronger in a myriad of ways.

NOTES

1. From White House budget request to Congress, cited in Jesse Jackson, "Invest in US Instead of Sacrificing in Iraq," *Chicago Sun-Times,* September 4, 2007.

2. NSHAPC, Rog, Shinn, and Culhane, 2003, from Dennis Culhane, *Family Homelessness: Where to From Here?* (2004), at www.endhomelessness.org/content/article/detail/1044.

3. W. Pitcoff, D. Pelletiere, S. Crowley, M. Treskon, and C. N. Dolbeare, *Out of Reach: 2004* (Washington, DC: The National Low Income Housing Coalition), available online at www.nlihc.org/oor2004/.

4. U.S. Department of Housing and Urban Development, Office of Policy Development and Research, *Trends in Worst Case Needs for Housing, 1978–1999: A report to Congress on worst case housing needs plus update on worst case needs in 2001* (2003).

5. M. Shin, B. C. Weitzman, D. Stojanovic, J. R. Knickman, L. Jimenez, L. Duchon, S. James, and D. H. Krantz, "Predictors of homelessness among families in New York City: From shelter request to housing stability," *American Journal of Public Health* 88 (11) (1998): 1561–1657.

6. www.nationalhomeless.org/publications/facts/veterans.html.

7. B. Sard, P. Lawrence, and W. Fischer, "Appropriations shortfall cuts funding for 80,000 housing vouchers this year: Congress rejected deeper reductions sought by Administration" (Washington, DC: Center on Budget and Policy Priorities), available online at www.cbpp.org/2-11-05hous.htm.

8. money.cnn.com/magazines/fortune/fortune_archive/2005/12/26/8364640/index.htm; also www.wired.com/wired/archive/7.09/stocktopia.html. ("His assumption this time is that the Dow Jones Industrial Average should show a 10 percent annual return for the next 26 years.")

9. Miloon Kothari, UN Press Briefing by Special Rapporteur on the Right to Adequate Housing, November 2005, online at www.un.org/News/briefings/docs/2005/kotharibrf050511.doc.htm.

10. www.habitat.org/how/factsheet.aspx

11. National Low Income Housing Coalition, online at www.nlihc.org/detail/article.cfm?article_id=2638&id=48.

12. Douglas Brinkley, "Reckless Abandonment," *The Washington Post,* August 26, 2007.

13. Institute for Southern Studies, *Southern Exposure—Blueprint for Gulf Renewal* (August/September 2007).

14. Nicolai Ouroussoff, "Two Infusions of Vision to Bolster New Orleans," *The New York Times*, August 28, 2007, online at www.nytimes.com/2007/08/28/arts/design/28jazz.html?_r=1&8dpc=&pagewanted=all&oref=slogin.

15. *Southern Exposure—Blueprint for Gulf Renewal*

16. Ibid.

17. Ibid.

18. Ibid.

19. swz.salary.com/salarywizard/layouthtmls/swzl_compresult_national_ LG 12000003.html

20. Bureau of Justice Statistics (BJS), *LEMAS Report.*

21. Survey conducted by Lake Research Partners for the National Voting Rights Institute, online at www.demos.org/pubs/VoterSurvey_010406.pdf.

22. Center for Responsive Politics, "'04 Elections Expected to Cost Nearly $4 Billion," online at www.opensecrets.org/pressreleases/2004/04spending.asp.

23. Joel Popkin and Company, *Small Business Share of Economic Growth,* final report submitted to U.S. Small Business Administration.

24. http://app1.sba.gov/faqs

25. National Federation of Independent Business Small-Business Poll, www .nfib.com/object/IO_34275.html.

26. T. W. Zimmerer and N. M. Scarborough, *Essentials of Entrepreneurship and Small Business Management,* 3rd ed. (Upper Saddle River, NJ: Prentice Hall, 2002).

27. Ibid.

28. M. J. Dollinger, *Entrepreneurship: Strategies and Resources*, 3rd ed. (Upper Saddle River, NJ: Prentice Hall, 2003).

29. "Entrepreneurs Expect Modest Startup Costs for Most New Ventures," www.sba.gov/advo/press/03-49.html.

30. http://search.sba.gov/highlight/index.html?url=http%3A//www.sba.gov/ad vo/stats/sbfaq.pdf&hltcol=sbaweb&term=startups&term=2006&term=649%2C700 &term=startups+2006+649%2C700&fterm=2006&la=en&charset=iso-8859-1& search=../query.html%3Fcharset%3Diso-8859-1%26col%3Dsbaweb%26qt%3Dstart ups%2B2006%2B649%252C700#ultraseek_hlt_0.

31. www.medicare.gov/LongTermCare/Static/Home.asp

32. www.pbs.org/newshour/bb/health/jan-june02/eden_2-27.html

33. Ibid.

34. Ibid.

35. www.health.state.mn.us/divs/chs/rhpc/PDFdocs/srhealth.pdf

36. www.indeed.com/salary?q1=chauffer&l1=

37. www.mbusa.com/models/main.do?modelCode=E350W

38. Based on Ibbotson forecast of market performance (see note 7).

39. www.americanprogress.org/issues/2007/05/air_cargo.html

40. Ibid.

41. "U.S. Senate 9/11 bill seeks more security aid, drops cargo inspection requirements," The Associated Press, February 13, 2007, online at www.iht.com/articles/ap/2007/02/14/america/NA-GEN-US-Congress-Terrorism.php.

42. www.americanprogress.org/issues/2007/05/air_cargo.html

43. *What Has Homeland Security Cost? An Assessment: 2001–2005* (Federal Reserve Bank of New York), online at www.newyorkfed.org/research/current_issues/ci13-2/ci13-2.html.

44. U.S. Congressional Research Service, as quoted online at www.alertnet.org/db/blogs/19216/2007/07/3-135555-1.htm.

45. Eric Lipton and Scott Shane, "Airline Security—Plot Shows Need for More

Passenger Data, Officials Say," *The New York Times,* August 15, 2006, online at www.nytimes.com/2006/08/15/world/europe/15visa.html?_r=1&oref=slogin

46. Report from the Committee on Oversight and Government Reform, online at oversight.house.gov/story.asp?ID=881.

47. http://democrats.senate.gov/dpc/dpc-new.cfm?doc_name=fs-109-2-56

48. Ibid.

49. Ibid.

50. Democratic Policy Committee Weekly National Security Index, April 11, 2006.

51. Marcia Merry Baker and Anita Gallagher, "Undercutting Veterans' Care Backfires on Bush/Cheney," *Executive Intelligence Review,* July 8, 2005, online at www.larouchepub.com/other/2005/3227bush_chisel_va.html.

52. Ibid.

53. H.R. 2642, the Military Construction and Veterans Affairs Appropriations Act, 2008, September 4, 2007.

54. "Keep VA Money for Veterans Care," *Rapid City Journal,* July 23, 2005, online at www.rapidcityjournal.com/articles/2005/07/23/news/opinion/opin120.txt.

55. U.S. Census Bureau, www.infoplease.com/spot/veteranscensus1.html.

56. H.R. 2642, the Military Construction and Veterans Affairs Appropriations Act, 2008, September 4, 2007.

57. U.S. Census Bureau press release, www.census.gov/Press-Release/www/releases/archives/voting/004986.html.

58. "Felony Disenfranchisement. The Sentencing Project," www.sentencing project.org/pdfs/1046.pdf.

59. National Academy of Social Insurance, www.nasi.org/usr_doc/Medicare_Brief_No_17.pdf.

60. Kaiser Family Foundation, "Medicare—a Primer," p. 13, March 2007, online at www.kaiserfamilyfoundation.org/medicare/upload/7615.pdf.

61. "Preventive Care: A National Profile on Use, Disparities, and Health Benefits," www.prevent.org/content/view/131/72/.

62. Partnership for Prevention, Congressional Briefing, September 20, 2007, online at www.prevent.org/content/view/129/72/.

63. Kaiser Family Foundation, 2007.

64. IMS Health, www.imshealth.com/ims/portal/front/articleC/0,2777,6599_3665_80415465,00.html.

65. Report from the Agency for Healthcare Research and Quality, as reported by CQ HealthBeat, posted at www.medicalnewstoday.com/articles/71944.php.

66. www.synergos.org/globalgivingmatters/features/0311harrison.htm

67. Average based on cost estimates for hospitals currently under construction or recently built in Qatar, Bangladesh, Saudi Arabia, Yemen, Nigeria, Gaza, and Afghanistan. www.gov.im/lib/docs/cso/annualreport20032004.pdf; http://daily .stanford.edu/article/2006/11/3/studentSeeksFundsForNigerianHospital; http://web .worldbank.org/external/projects; www.synergos.org/globalgivingmatters/features/ 0311harrison.htm; http://english.people.com.cn/200308/02/eng20030802_121562 .shtml; Iran Daily, Feb. 3, 2007, www.iran-daily.com/1385/2772/pdf/i8.pdf; and http://domino.un.org/unispal.nsf/f45643a78fcba719852560f6005987ad/cd46e1cac 8268870852560fd005af13c!OpenDocument.

68. http://daily.stanford.edu/article/2006/11/3/student SeeksFundsForNigerian Hospital

69. www.cia.gov/library/publication/the-world-factbook/geos/xx.html#people.

70. WSIS 2005 (World Summit of Information) Tunis 2005, online at www.itu .int/wsis/tunis/newsroom/stats/index.html.

71. Ibid.

72. Wireless Internet for the City of Berkeley, www.ci.berkeley.ca.us/city council/2006citycouncil/packet/072506/2006-07-25%20Item%2043%20Wireless %20Internet.pdf.

73. www.citymayors.com/statistics/largest-cities-population-125.html

74. "World's Largest Cities (Ranked by City Population)," www.mongabay .com/cities_pop_03.htm.

75. World population taken from CIA *World Factbook*, www.cia.gov/library/ publications/the-world-factbook/geos/xx.html#people; family size taken from UNFPA (United Nations Population Fund), *State of World Population 2004*, www .unfpa.org/swp/2004/english/ch1/page7.htm.

76. CIA *World Factbook*, www.cia.gov/library/publications/the-world-factbook/ geos/xx.html#people.

77. U.S. Agency for International Development, from a speech at the National Press Club, as reported by UPI, February 24, 2006, online at www.rebuild-iraq -expo.com/newsdetails05.asp?id=2036.

78. Central Intelligence Agency, *The World Factbook,* online at www.cia.gov/ library/publications/the-world-factbook/geos/xx.html#Intro.

79. www.cia.gov/library/publications/the-world-factbook/geos/xx.html#people

80. Based on household statistics from www.gov.pe.ca/photos/original/ pt_annualreview.pdf and averages of real estate listings found online at www.all anweeks.com and www.coldwellbanker.com/servlet/News?action=viewNewsItem &contentId=700726&customerType=News.

81. Jeanne Sahadi, "CEO Pay: 364 Times More Than Workers'," CNNMoney .com, August 29, 2007, online at www.truthout.org/issues_06/082907LA.shtml.

82. Ibid.

83. Michael Santoli, "Rich America, Poor America," Today from Barron's, on-line at www.smartmoney.com/barrons/index.cfm?story=20070123.

84. Ibid.

85. Ibid.

86. As of December 26, 2007, online at www.census.gov/population/www/ popclockus.html.

87. 2007 OASDI trustees report, online at www.ssa.gov/OACT/TR/TR07/II_ project.html#wp105057.

88. David Hogberg, "The True Cost of Social Security," *The American Spectator,* April 19, 2005, online at www.spectator.org.

89. www.populationeducation.org/docs/300millionlessons/usapopclock.pdf

90. consumerist.com

91. Ibid.

92. Ibid.

93. abcnews.com

94. American Bankruptcy Institute, "Bankruptcy Filings During First Half Of 2006 Fall to Lowest Levels Since 1986," online at www.abiworld.org/AM/Template .cfm?Section=Home&TEMPLATE=/CM/ContentDisplay.cfm&CONTENTID=42654.

95. U.S. Department of Commerce, Bureau of the Census, www.census.gov/ prod/1/pop/p25-1129.pdf.

96. Center on Budget and Policy Priorities, online at www.cbpp.org/4-14-04tax -sum.htm.

97. Ibid.

98. Ibid.

99. Regarding the Tax Fairness and Fiscal Policy Effects of the Bush Tax Cuts, March 5, 2007, online at www.ctj.org/pdf/housetestimony030507.pdf (p. 3).

100. Isaac Shapiro, "Deficit Dance," *The Washington Post*, January 11, 2005, online at www.washingtonpost.com/wp-dyn/articles/A64428-2005Jan10.html.

101. Ibid.

102. CTJ Citizens for Tax Justice, April 2007, online at www.ctj.org/pdf/oecd07 .pdf.

103. Isaac Shapiro, "Deficit Dance," *The Washington Post*.

104. "On This Tax Day, Push for Reform," April 16, 2007, online at www .americanprogress.org/issues/2007/04/tax_day.html.

105. Economic Policy Institute, online at www.epinet.org/content.cfm?id=2777.

106. Census Bureau data, cited at http://uspolitics.about.com/b/2007/09/03/labor-day-facts-data.htm.

107. www.accessmylibrary.com

108. Ibid.

109. *The Epoch Times,* May 2–8, 2007, online at daikynguyen.com/eet/print_archive/australia/national/2007/05_May/Edition%20121/Edition%20121%20page09.pdf.

110. Ibid.

111. Census Bureau data, cited at http://uspolitics.about.com/b/2007/09/03/labor-day-facts-data.htm.

112. U.S. Dept. of Energy, online at www.energy.gov/energysources/electric power.htm

113. revelle.net/lakeside/lakeside.new/understanding.html

114. "Green Dreams," *National Geographic,* October 2007, p. 40.

115. James R. Healey, "Is Ethanol the Answer?" www.usatoday.com/money/industries/technology/2006-02-01-ethanol_x.htm.

116. "Ethanol and the Local Community" (AUS Consultants and SJH & Company, 2002).

117. U.S. plants produced 4 billion gallons last year. That's only enough to replace 3% of the 140 billion gallons of gasoline the USA burned last year. (www.usatoday.com/tech/science/2006-02-01-ethanol_x.htm)

118. Michael Wang, Argonne National Laboratories, as quoted at www .harvestcleanenergy.org/enews/enews_0505/enews_0505_cellulosic_ethanol.htm.

119. "Switch," *Wired* magazine, October 2007, p. 160.

120. www.harvestcleanenergy.org/enews/enews_0505/enews_0505_cellulosic _ethanol.htm

121. From a speech by Eileen Claussen, president, Pew Center on Global Climate Change at the Institute of Transportation Studies, University of California, Davis, May 3, 2001, online at www.pewclimate.org/press_room/speech_transcripts/transcript_transport335.cfm.

122. www.usatoday.com/tech/news/2006-03-12-ethanol-boom_x.htm

123. Idaho Dept. of Environmental Quality, online at www.deq.idaho.gov/air/prog_issues/pollutants/vehicles_hybrid.cfm.

124. "Toyota's US Sales of Prius and Camry Hybrids Soared in March," online at www.greencarcongress.com/2007/04/toyotas_us_sale.html.

125. www.toyota.com/camry/specs.html

126. www.smartmoney.com

127. National Independent Automobile Dealers Association, www.niada.com/Industry_Information/ind_bhph.htm.

128. www.census.gov/prod/2006pubs/p23-209.pdf, p.1

129. Department of Transportation records, as cited in Kathleen Murphy, "Elderly drivers pose policy-making challenge," Stateline.org, April 29, 2004, online at www.stateline.org/live/ViewPage.action?siteNodeId=136&languageId=1&contentId=15633.

130. "Build Your Buick," online at www.buick.com/byo/selectColor.bk?styleId=CX%20&style=CX%20&pvc=471&make=Buick&zip=48226&noType=0&makeId=004&model=LaCrosse&subModelId=242&year=2007&modelId=077&brand=lacrosse&originatingBrand=divisional&contexLink=.

131. "Build Your Buick," online at www.buick.com/byo/buildSummary.bk;jsessionid=V1NVDTARGCXKQCQN1ECSCZQKBXMQEIMO?regularOptions=PCI^K05^US9^CF5^P31&iPi=3&fPi=3&pvc=424&exteriorColor=Black%20Onyx%20&colorOptions=41U^393^A51&interiorColorId=393&styleId=CXS%20&make=Buick&seatTypeId=A51&model=Lucerne&modelId=095&noType=0&exteriorColorId=41U&year=2007&interiorColor=Cocoa/cashmere%20Custom%20Perforated%20Leather-appointed%20Seats%20&colorVisited=true&subModelId=298&makeId=004&style=CXS%20&zip=48226&&vehicleModel=/images/gmbp/11004/vehicle/2007/med/298_8555.jpg&contexLink=&originatingBrand=DIVISIONAL&regionid=.

132. www.autosavant.net

133. www.citystages.org/

134. Greater Birmingham Convention and Visitors Bureau, online at citystages.org/sustain/faq.html.

135. Brian Mosely, "Bonnaroo Has Huge Economic Impact," Shelbyville, TN *Times-Gazette*, June 8, 2006, online at www.t-g.com/story/1155871.html.

136. Austin Music Commission report.

137. Mark Scott, "Peace, Love, and Corporate Sponsorship," *BusinessWeek*, August 13, 2007.

138. Study conducted by Universal Orlando Resort, online at www.wsbtv.com/money/4534923/detail.html.

139. www.zagat.com/about/about.aspx?menu=PR12

140. www.fodors.com/wire/archives/001379.cfm

141. Ida Byrd-Hill, "Avoid After Vacation Stress," online at: ezinearticles.com/?Avoid-After-Vacation-Stress&id=74688.

142. www.census.gov/compendia/statab

143. *The Times*, March 26, 2005, online at: www.timesonline.co.uk/tol/news/world/article437699.ece.

144. College Board study, online at www.collegeboard.com/parents/csearch/know-the-options/21385.html.

145. U.S. Census Bureau, online at nces.ed.gov/fastfacts/display.asp?id=65.

146. The Heritage Foundation, online at www.heritage.org.

147. Ibid.

148. The Heritage Foundation, online at www.heritage.org/Research/Education/wm478.cfm#q6.

149. Martin Crutsinger, "Factory Jobs: 3 Million Lost Since 2000," AP, April 20, online at www.breitbart.com/article.php?id=D8OKGR480&show_article=1.

150. David Kusnet, "Labor's Search for Job Security," online at multinationalmonitor.org/hyper/issues/1987/11/kusnet.html.

151. Crutsinger, "Factory Jobs: 3 Million Lost Since 2000."

152. Ibid.

153. educationusa.state.gov/finaid.htm

154. American Council for Drug Education, www.acde.org/common/Tobacco .htm.

155. "Changing Risk Behaviors and Addressing Environmental Challenges," The Community Guide, www.thecommunityguide.org/tobacco/Tobacco.pdf.

156. Ibid.

157. Kerry Cavanaugh, "Prop. O would aid cleanup of river, Santa Monica Bay," Daily News, October 18, 2004, online at: www.theriverproject.org/DailyNewsPropO .pdf.

158. www.austinmonorail.org/monorail_costs.htm

159. Tom Weeks, "Encouraging lessons from the Vegas monorail," The Seattle Times, online at archives.seattletimes.nwsource.com/cgi-bin/texis. cgi/web/vortex/ display?slug=weeksop15&date=20020115.

160. Omar Sofradzija, "Mass transit alternatives moving along smoothly," Las Vegas Review-Journal, June 6, 2004, online at www.rtcsouthernnevada.com/max/ pressroom/articles/june0604.pdf.

161. wilshiremonorail.net/MonorailVsSubway.htm

162. health.msn.com/reports/obesity

163. Ibid.

164. Centers for Disease Control and Prevention, online at www.cdc.gov/ nccdphp/dnpa/obesity/faq.htm.

165. Ibid.

166. U.S. Census, www.census.gov/prod/1/popp25-1129pdf.

167. M. Woolley and S. Propst, "Public Attitudes and Perceptions About Health-Related Research," The Journal of the American Medical Association 294 (September 21, 2005): 1380–84.

168. Frank R. Lichtenberg, "The Expanding Pharmaceutical Arsenal in the War on Cancer," National Bureau of Economic Research Working Paper No. 10328 (Cambridge, MA: NBER, February 2004)

169. nih.gov/about/nihoverview

170. H. Moses, E. Dorsey, D. Matheson, and S. Their, "Financial anatomy of biomedical research," The Journal of the American Medical Association 294 (11): 1333–42.

171. www.innovation.org/index.cfm/InnovationToday/KeyIssues/Innovation _at_a_Crossroads

172. Deroy Murdock, "Pills Don't Grow on Trees," National Review Online, www.nationalreview.com/murdock/murdock200411290832.asp.

173. Ibid.

174. Alan Riding, "A Gleaming New Guggenheim for Grimy Bilbao," The New York Times, June 24, 1997, online at query.nytimes.com/gst/fullpage.html?sec= travel&res=9D06E6D91F3EF937A15755C0A961958260&fta=y.

175. www.fhwa.dot.gov/ohim/hs01/hm41.htm

176. www.JerrysArtarama.com

177. www.transalt.org/blueprint/chapter4/chapter4b.html

178. CityMayors statistics, online at www.citymayors.com/gratis/uscities_200 .html.

179. U.S. Department of Justice, Bureau of Labor Statistics, www.ojp.usdoj .gov/bjs/prisons.htm.

180. Center on Juvenile and Criminal Justice, "Poor Prescription: The Costs of Imprisoning Drug Offenders in the United States," online at www.cjcj.org/pubs/ poor/pp.html.

181. Paige M. Harrison and Allen J. Beck, Ph.D., U.S. Department of Justice, Bureau

of Statistics, Prisoners in 2005 (Washington, DC: U.S. Department of Justice, November 2006), p.10, Table 14.

182. *US Department of Justice, Bureau of Justice Statistics, Federal Criminal Case Processing, 2000, with Trends 1982–2000* (Washington, DC: US Department of Justice, November 2001), p. 12, Table 6

183. www.reuters.com/article/idUSNO868808320070508

184. Bryan Bender, "Analysis says war could cost $1 trillion," *The Boston Globe,* August 1, 2007, online at www.boston.com/news/nation/articles/2007/08/01/analysis_says_war_could_cost_1_trillion.

185. Tom Regan, "Report: Iraq War Costs Could Top $2 Trillion," *The Christian Science Monitor,* online at www.csmonitor.com/2006/0110/dailyUpdate.html.